The Way We Wore

Styles of the 1930s and '40s

and Our World Since Then

The Way We Wore

Styles of the 1930s and '40s
and Our World Since Then

Shown and Recalled

By

Marsha Hunt

Fallbrook
Publishing, Ltd.

Publisher's Note

Striving to preserve the reproduction quality of
Marsha Hunt's rare film collection, as well as her
writings, this First Edition is printed on
acid free paper to prevent yellowing.
A few photographs are reprinted from old newspapers
or magazines, resulting in a different facsimile quality.
We feel their historical significance requires inclusion.

Seemingly uncommon abbreviations or usage of
words, where found, are original photo captions and
news copy. No revisions are made for today's standards.

Produced and Published by

Fallbrook Publishing, Ltd.

Robert Francis Laktas & Dirk Wayne Summers, Founders
Dirk W. Summers, CEO
Robert F. Laktas, Managing Editor, Emeritus
1119 South Mission Road, Suite 362
Fallbrook, California 92028
(619) 940-8500   Fax (619) 940-8900

Production Manager: Chris Jones
Project Editors: Corene Boettcher Adams,
William Kortsch, Lillian C. Zenz.

Dustcover, book layout and typesetting
designed and produced by
Chris Jones, Riverside, California

Film work and lithographic reproductions
supervised by
Salvador T. Sanchez, Colorscan Systems
San Diego, California

This First Edition printed and bound in the United States of America

7   6   5   4   3   2   1

ISBN 1-882747-00-3
Library of Congress Catalog Card Number 92-83890

Front and back cover photos by Virgil Apger, MGM

Acknowledgment

An old and valued friend has breathed life into a project I have been working on for some years. His faith in this book, and me, has finally brought "The Way We Wore" into print. A documentary filmmaker, he spent the past two years becoming a book publisher, in order to give "The Way We Wore" its chance.

If it weren't for Dirk Summers, you would not be reading these words, or perusing these pictures. My gratitude to him is immense, as is my affection.

Marsha Hunt
Sherman Oaks, California

Part One

The Thirties

Part Two

The Forties

Introduction

"A Sweeter Day," many have called it, the time span we refer to as the '30s and '40s. At best, bittersweet, many would add, and some would insist that it is absurd to refer to the decades that subjected Americans to the Great Depression and World War II as anything like sweet. And yet I believe that for all the stress and suffering those years undeniably brought, there was indeed a kind of sweetness in them, too.

We still had our innocence as a people, we cherished and stuck by our families and our friends, and neighbors were neighborly. When faced with a challenge, a problem or even tragedy, we simply coped. We clung to our belief that effort and good would be rewarded, sloth and evil punished, and to our belief in the happy ending. Those convictions and that blind faith were nourished by the movies we all attended regularly as escape, diversion and inspiration.

For me, those years were sweet beyond my wildest imaginings. The first half of the '30s was spent growing up and going to school in New York City. Graduating at 16 from the excellent Horace Mann School for Girls, and determined to become an actress, I enrolled in a dramatic school, Theodora Irvine's Studio for the Theater. Partly to help pay the cost of tuition, and partly to learn about cameras, lighting, make-up, grooming and such, I also became a model with the famed John Powers Agency. Being tall and reed slim, I naturally fell into fashion work more than any other kind.

1

Within a year - June of 1935 and at age 17- I was in Hollywood, under contract to Paramount Pictures and given nothing but lead roles right from the start! It was astonishing good luck. The studio Publicity Department had a problem with me, though, because I refused to pose for the mandatory "cheese-cake, leg-art" kind of photos that were expected of all young-girl contractees. I meant to be a serious actress, and bathing beauty cuteness collided with my hopes and self-image. Also, though I never admitted it, I knew that my long, lean and here-and-there bony body would look pathetic, exposed.

In desperation, then, the publicity boys decided that since I had been a fashion model, and they had to publicize me somehow, I might as well pose for fashion layouts during my days off from shooting films. And so it happened that I posed in hundreds and hundreds of current styles, the pictures going forth to magazines and newspapers all over the world. It may well be that I did more fashion posing than any other actress in those days.

When I began my seven-year stint at MGM Studios in 1939, it was somewhat the same but less prolific because I was kept so busy making films that there wasn't much time left for publicity work. The latter '40s were spent as a free lance at various studios and in New York where I shot a film and made the transition to the Broadway stage. Those years, too, brought occasional fashion posing.

I've lived in the same house since 1946, through 40 years of marriage and 7 of widowhood. When my husband and I moved in, we found a closet behind the laundry room where we stored our mountainous piles of radio and film scripts, and my envelopes of studio publicity pictures, to get them out of the way and out of harm's way, just in case we'd ever want to look at them again. In all that time, our lives were too busy for backward looking, until recently.

I served as honorary chairman of the benefit premiere of a huge new shopping complex, the Galleria in Sherman Oaks, and the theme of the event was the films of the '30s and '40s. Recalling all those old fashion shots from just that period, I hauled them out and selected some for an exhibit. The interest and scrutiny they aroused were a heartening surprise and gave birth to the idea for this book of pictures and comments.

Some are costumes I wore in films, and a few are wardrobe tests, complete with the descriptive slate beside me. Some are from my own wardrobe. Many, though, are simply outfits brought in for me to model for publicity fashion pictures, and it's far too late for me to credit all the designers or the stores where they originated. I'm including, as well, production stills from scenes in (then) contemporary movies, where the style was interesting, and I hadn't done a fashion still shot. There are also some snaps out on dates or at parties where style trends of those times can be noted.

Following the clothes sections on each decade, you'll find a section on hats and hairstyles. You'll notice that several trends and fads of the day are missing, but not intentionally so, just because I have no picture of them. Nearly all the photographs in this book, remember, came out of that forgotten closet. You'll simply be taking fashion potluck. I found a few production stills I didn't own, at the Academy of Motion Picture Arts and Sciences' Library. And I'm also indebted to that most devoted and diligent of fans, Bev Montalbano, for having sent me, before she died, her enormous scrapbooks from which I've lifted some appropriate clippings. I don't think she'd have minded sharing them with you.

Neither bizarre nor extreme, the clothes shown here are a fair retrospective of styles of that period, reflecting what comfortably situated women actually were wearing then, with only here and there a touch of splendor. Not too much high style, in other words, to be a fairly faithful wearing apparel record of the time.

Please remember though, no fashion nor writing expert, I! With neither training nor experience in the field of fashion, I've simply noticed and enjoyed wearing a great many different styles over the years and want to share them with you, along with my highly personal opinions, observations and recollections of those times. Included in these will be some memories of my two weddings, of the Roosevelt White House, the Hollywood Canteen, the frozen reaches of the Arctic, and of Hollywood's first exposure to political inquisition and blacklists, as milestones of my experience during those years, that might be of interest.

It's embarrassing, to be in every single picture here. They're simply what I had to work with. At least you'll find a number of old favorite players here and there, along with my everpresent face! Let's hope that in time others will provide you with the multiple star dress parade the subject deserves. This collection, therefore, is presented, not as a bookful of me, but as a reminder of how we all were and *wore*, and to point out how much we're reverting half a century later, at least in some clothing aspects, to that sweeter day.

Part One

The Thirties

Clothing
Key to a Type or Time

Consciously or not, we choose the clothes we wear to reflect an impression we have (or wish we had) of ourselves, an impression we'd like others to have of us. Our clothing becomes a kind of self-presentation, to be read at a glance by the people around us. Abetted by our chosen hairstyle and make-up (or the absence of any) our clothing helps us come across as mature or youthful, conservative or daring, sophisticated or ingenuous, bookish or sporty, neat or sloppy, distinctive or nondescript, modest or flamboyant, fragile or sturdy, original or conforming. Quite a responsibility, clothes shopping, or just choosing what to wear each day.

And just as our clothes tell others a lot about ourselves from day to day, so the prevailing styles of recent decades tell us much about those times. ❧

The Twenties

As Prelude

In the 1920s, nationwide relief that World War I was over erupted in a kind of prolonged "Wheeeeee!" Women sheared off their tresses into "bobs," (hair worn short and close to the head). There were even boyish bobs. As more and more city women emerged from their homes to board buses, trolleys and subways that took them to work in offices, shops and factories, they refused the hobbling confinement of long skirts. And once they started raising hemlines, they got carried away and raised them clear above the knees, becomingly or not. Having won their long-denied right to vote in 1920, women felt emancipated indeed, and rebelled against their wasp-waist corsets. By mid-decade, they asserted all-out freedom from any waistline at all and defiantly placed their belts and sashes down around their hips! Further, they abandoned their softly feminine, bosomy look, preferring to appear as flat-chested as possible. This came more easily to some than to others, and some of the best-endowed actually bound their busts. A grotesque period, but they were having fun.

This revolution in women's appearance was less militant than good-natured. If they were no longer wilting, clinging vines, they now chose to be pert, peppy and cute. Oh, there were also the "vamps," slinking about with long cigarette holders, but even they must have known they were a put-on, "being" blasé sophisticates. They sported cloche hats obscuring their eyebrows, long rope pearl necklaces, T-strap sandals and buckled pumps, beaded and fringed formals, marabou feathers and monkey fur. In their boudoirs, leggy French dolls lolled against lace-covered satin pillows, drenched in seductive scent. (Don't tell me they weren't giggling inside!)

Prohibition, also launched in 1920, simply provided a challenge of how to get around it, and thus were born bathtub gin, speakeasies, bootlegging and organized crime in the land of the free. Nightclubs, jazz (wailing saxophones and rinky-tink banjos), the Charleston, ocean liners, mah-jongg, collegiate football, raccoon coats, rumble seats and the sky's-the-limit stock market. All were part of the Wheeeeee! decade, then, near its end, came the Crash. 🍏

The Thirties

The wet blanket the Great Depression threw over the nation's long wild party was reflected in changes of style. Down came the hemlines to mid and lower calf, back up to the waist came the belts, as we all tightened them. Life was real, life was earnest, and we dressed accordingly. Oh, the high style ladies still looked pretty striking, but most of us dressed much more quietly and modestly. Colors were subdued, lines more natural and less extreme. Gowns cut on the bias even gave a kind of droopy look. In general, except for such lifts to the spirit as the Empress Eugénie hat, the fact is, we looked a little dowdy, a little mousey. That lasted for about the first half of the '30s, while the nation reeled under bank failures, foreclosed mortgages, bankruptcies, unemployment, breadlines, soup kitchens and dust bowls. A grimly testing time for Americans, and we looked it.

Movies, on the other hand, were quite another matter. Recognizing the public's need of relief from gloom, for some escape and fantasy, Hollywood provided just that. Gloom was routed by guffaws at the inspired antics of Laurel and Hardy, Charlie Chaplin, Harold Lloyd, the Marx Brothers, W. C. Fields and more. Escape of every kind was provided, with a spectrum of fare from horror and fright *(Dracula, Frankenstein, Dr. Jekyll and Mr.*

Hyde, King Kong); to romance *(Smilin' Through, Back Street, Berkeley Square, The Barretts of Wimpole Street);* to detecting *(Sherlock Holmes, Bulldog Drummond);* to crime and gangland *(Little Caesar, Public Enemy, Scarface);* to spectacle *(Cleopatra, Sign of the Cross);* to war *(All Quiet on the Western Front, Journey's End, Hell's Angels);* to history and adventure *(Disraeli, The Private Life of Henry VIII, Svengali, Cimarron, Rasputin and the Empress, Trader Horn, Viva Villa!);* to filmed novels and plays *(Moby Dick, Little Women, A Farewell to Arms, Arrowsmith, Rain, The Guardsman, The Front Page, Dinner at Eight, Holiday, Of Human Bondage);* to assorted delights such as *(Cavalcade, She Done Him Wrong, Tarzan the Ape Man, Morning Glory, Grand Hotel, The Thin Man, and It Happened One Night),* all served up by Hollywood to a needful and gratefully relishing public during those darkest Depression years of the early mid-'30s. These are just samplings, to say nothing of that new delight ushered in with sound: musicals.

For true fantasy at a time of pervasive poverty, there were drawing room comedies, with madcap adventures of the very rich, all in mansions and yachts and limousines and nightclubs, with scads of servants, and all dressed to the teeth in the richest, divinest creations a memorable corps of studio designers and sometimes even Paris couturiers could devise. Thus, for a dime, quarter or fifty cents, eked out of pathetically shrunken budgets, we fed our national weekly habit of moviegoing and clung to that lifeline of hope for a better day.

Scholars and sociologists can tell us to how great an extent the movies we saw shaped our morals, our dreams and ambitions, our impressions of history and the world, our customs, slang and taste, but we don't need anyone, however, to tell us what an influence movies have had on how we dress.

The bearers of glad rag tidings in the mid-1930s were such as Constance Bennett, Merle Oberon, Kay Francis, Helen Vinson, Marlene Dietrich, Carole Lombard, Myrna Loy, Claudette Colbert, Irene Dunne, Rosalind Russell and, oh indeed, Joan Crawford - as sleek, svelte and gorgeous an array of fashion missionaries as ever was seen. What they wore, we copied as best we could. They epitomized high fashion on the screen. We began to learn the names of designers for the screen: Travis Banton, Orry-Kelly, Howard Greer, Edith Head, Walter Plunkett, Omar Kyam. One designer, Adrian at MGM, changed women's silhouettes throughout the western world by capitalizing on Joan Crawford's broad shoulders and slim hips. What a way to look! The rest of us squared and padded our shoulders for more than a decade, and we did our best to diet and exercise away our rounded hips.

One memorable day, newspaper front pages across the land carried a picture of the glamour queen, blonde and seductive import Marlene Dietrich as she had appeared at a festive Hollywood event, garbed in a perfectly tailored and astonishingly becoming tuxedo suit, trousers and all, just like a man's! The nation rocked with laughter and clucked with shock at her "unwomanliness," but there was no little envy among women at how marvelous she looked in trousers, even relaxed and assured as well. Very soon after, the charismatic and spiritedly independent new star Katharine Hepburn showed up in public wearing well-tailored pants, and looking as if she and they were made for each other. The rage was on and rages still. Slacks, as they soon were named, became part of every woman's wardrobe - a huge mistake for the huge, of whom we have many. The freedom of movement, the casual feeling they give, won all women's hearts, and bottoms.

Through the '30s and until World War II, slacks were usually confined to casual wear for most of us. Daytime garb for women who worked or went shopping or lunched with friends usually was a dress, an ensemble (a dress with a matching jacket which could be short as a bolero or as long as a tunic) or a well-tailored suit. This would be topped by furs or coat, as weather dictated. And were usually set off by a hat and gloves, besides the essential purse. Thus, the total effect was of an outfit, an assemblage of items that looked well together. Color coordinating or even matching of shades took time in the finding, but paid off in the net effect.

By about 1935, when I began in motion pictures and this collection of photographs also began, that rather dowdy skirt length was creeping upward to around mid-calf. By the late '30s, hemlines hovered becomingly at upper-calf. Variety and a bit more zing came into our styles, reflecting our gradual emergence from the long Depression. 🐦

Fashions in Modeling

My recollection of the fashion shows I did in '34 and '35 is that we models strove for elegance, grace and fluidity of movement. We took long, smooth strides to the appointed spot, swiveled on the balls of both feet to face the other way, the now-forward foot pointed with infinite grace in the new direction, stood still a magic second for the sheer wonder of what we were wearing to sink in on the lucky viewers, then lifted the pointed-forward foot to start the glide on the way back. Oh, it was leisurely. It had gentle disdain, and sought to convey that anyone wearing this particular design was wrapped in the ultraconfidence of looking perfect.

Now and then, we permitted ourselves a small smile, even a mischievous twinkle, as we swept our gaze over those assembled. When the outfit was casual or sporty, we strode about, flashing breezy, friendly smiles. The smash hit musical "Roberta" was playing currently, with its spectacular fashion show, highlighted and made memorable by its accompanying Jerome Kern song, "Lovely to Look At." If you had seen that musical on both stage and screen, as I had, and then modelled in a fashion show, you moved about, imbued with all the glamour and magic of what you'd watched and heard.

I suppose we all slunk a bit, the "debutante slouch" being then in great vogue. This meant caving in your chest, raising your shoulders slightly, and shoving your pelvis forward. It felt and looked marvelously careless and languid. It was exemplified by Constance Bennett, then reigning on the screen for sheer chic and glamorous beauty, and currently the highest paid of all film stars, with a breathtaking $30,000 each and every week. Single-handedly, that lovely lady ruined my posture for years.

Since fashion shows, fashion magazines and the entire women's clothing business are predicated on change from season to season, it's inevitable that styles in the <u>modeling</u> of clothes should evolve and change, too. In the decades since the mid '30s, we've seen many different approaches to the showing of clothes. The shows I've seen lately are choreographed - literally - the models zingy and often doing their own disco thing to disco music. It's fun to watch, of course, and moves along at a breathless pace, but I'm not sure that we viewers absorb the styles as much as the models and the action.

Then there was the period when models scuttled with both knees bent, taking small, mincing steps. The mid-calf length of tight, tight skirts dictated that. Before long, with miniskirts, came the angular period - elbows out and arms akimbo, legs starkly apart, the net effect, strident and unfeminine. Lately I've seen lovely models in shows and "print ads," sullenly staring out at their public with looks of challenge and outright hostility. I think they think they're being sexy. Luckily, such fads not only come - but go. ❦

Making Fashion Pictures

Posing for fashion photographers certainly has seen its different phases, too. In fact, the very term "posing" is obsolete today, as models twist and turn, lean, leap and spin, toss their heads, wave their arms, and seem never to be still for a moment, while the photographers keep up a rapid-fire camera clicking that would shame a machine gun. Motion. Today all is camera-captured motion, much of it quite wonderful and effective, what with swinging hair, swirling skirts and scarves. I do find myself wondering sometimes how an outfit so photographed might look, if one were so revolutionary as simply to stand still in it, or even sit. That's what prospective buyers would do, most of the time. Today a model <u>moves</u> for a fashion photo layout.

We posed. Every fashion picture in this collection, except for the walking shots, was posed, fabric wrinkles smoothed, the best angle sought, for showing the garment at its best. Every indoor sitting was lighted with painstaking care, and once one's "pose" was determined, the challenge was to hold it forever if need be, and keep the facial expression fresh, until all was just right for the eventual single camera click.

By today's standards, the pictures shown here must amount to a period piece. They did show off the clothes, though. And the old method sure saved a lot of wasted film. ❦

13

Models In Movies

In 1936, when I was a year into my contract, Paramount signed three more New York fashion models, and gathered us for publicity stills.

Elizabeth Russell, Veda Ann Borg, Louise Stuart and I step bravely off into the future, flanking Paramount's resident distinguished-English-gentleman-actor, dashing Sir Guy Standing.

The other shot can have only one possible caption: "Starting their climb on the ladder to fame": M.H., Veda Ann Borg, Elizabeth Russell and Louise Stuart.

Background is the studio dressing room building, with stars on the first floor, featured and supporting players above. That could well be my proud first car in the far background, a Plymouth coupe.

Some other prominent models who came briefly to motion pictures around that time were Gwili André, Marguerite Chapman, Betty Wyman and Anita Colby, and soon after, one who stayed around much longer, Lauren Bacall. 🍎

15

The Studio Photographers

As gifted in their field as the great cameramen in the Golden Age of films, were the studio photographers. The debt we players owe them is just incalculable. Most of them quiet, unflappable artist/technicians, they daily transformed our mere mortal faces into dreamlike visions. With nothing but lights and their own talents, they flattered us all immeasurably, while managing to distill whatever was distinctive about each one's features, bone structure, expression and personality, to set each apart from all others, as unique. After being shown the results of a portrait sitting with its final retouching, it was always a shock, the next time I faced a mirror as God made me.

Each major studio had its chief photographer, responsible for portraits, poster stills, fashion and special layouts. During my stay at Paramount, that was gifted Eugene Robert Richee, and at Metro, the legendary Clarence Sinclair Bull. Others I recall posing for in the gallery or on the set were William Walling, Virgil Apger, Don English and Willinger, who used but one name. At RKO, I remember Ernest Bachrach.

Virtually every posed photo you'll see in this book was taken by one of the above, along with some others whose names have left me, even if visual proof of their skill has not.

At both Paramount and MGM, the Still Galleries were modest-sized bungalows with small name plates to identify them. But through their portals passed every great star and contract player, as well as all "name" freelance actors and those on loan-out from other studios, working on the lot.

After a photo session, we usually were given a set of the finally selected pictures for publication, as a reward for our pains, and those sessions could be long, hot and tiring. This is how I happened to amass enough prints from my fashion sittings to fill this book. 🐦

John Engstead

Our Paramount Still Gallery had an Art Director, a touch of class I don't believe any other studio provided, and he was a delight. John Engstead, tall, blonde and handsome as any leading man, brought a zest and sense of fun to his work, along with a keen eye and flawless taste.

He planned the theme of each photo session, chased down the wanted furnishings, draperies and props - in short, he "dressed the set." He helped choose what would be worn and with what accessories; then, somehow not stepping on the photographer's toes (he was busy, anyway, setting the lights), Engstead would coax, kid or even con the player/subject into the mood, attitude or expression desired. I believe he was the first to bring a photo session out-of-doors.

An inspired gossip and raconteur, "Steady," as I named him, and I became great friends, but never a romance. His heart was hopelessly elsewhere. We went together to previews and parties.

I often felt he should be taking the photos himself, and finally he did set up his own studio in Beverly Hills, enjoying great success as a portraitist. In the late '40s he shot a layout on me at the beach for Harper's Bazaar. It was cold, damp and windy, but he made it fun, and so were the pictures.

Before his death a few years ago, he published a book of portraits and reminiscences called "Star Shots," that is charming.

"Steady" and Gene Richee both should be credited for most of the Paramount fashion shots from the 1930s. ❧

John Engstead and I enter a theater to attend a film preview. It must have been a movie of mine, because bringing up the rear is my often-dated dentist, Dr. Eugene Dyer, who looked distractingly like Errol Flynn. (But there the resemblance ended)

Pictures of '30s Fashions

1930s Suits

Pretty contemporary, wouldn't you say? Except maybe for the gloves - mandatory accessories then.

Press caption:

HOLLYWOOD'S FAVORITE COSTUME - for fall is shown here on Marsha Hunt, Paramount player now in *"The Accusing Finger."* An oxford gray tailleur, handmade French blouse of white crepe, a jewelled clip, smart felt hat with vivid wisp of feather and carefully chosen accessories make this outfit one hundred percent in autumn chic.

P1085-349

Those epaulettes topping slightly puffed shoulders were a special touch. And the strapped spectator pumps are back today at about eight times the 1936 price tag - as what isn't?

Press caption:

BEIGE AND BROWN - an ideal combination for the fall sports costume Marsha Hunt, Paramount player in "*The Accusing Finger*," wears here, - a smart two-piece frock of beige jersey with padded shoulders, patch pockets and a smooth brown leather belt, which matches the novel leather buttons on the jacket. A brown felt hat and one-strap brown walking shoes complete the costume.

Copr. 1936, Paramount Production, Inc.

Just lift that hem a few inches, and I'd wear it today.

Press caption:

A brown, white-and-red flecked tweed suit, trimmed with red buttons, belt and scarf. The swagger coat is of red wool, worn with brown hat, gloves and oxfords.

Copr. 1936, Paramount Production, Inc.

"College Holiday" in 1936, was a musical romp with Jack Benny, George Burns and Gracie Allen and Martha Raye - only a few of a great array of comics. Leif Ericson and I sang to each other on a dance floor, in a gondola and in a tree.

Copr. 1936, Paramount Production, Inc.

Press caption:

WHEN SPRING BREAKS THROUGH AGAIN - suits like this will reign supreme in feminine style circles. Marsha Hunt, Paramount player in "*College Holiday*," likes the double coat the suit boasts. The skirt is brown wool topped by brown and white checks for both the jacket and its box coat with roomy patch pockets. A soft brown crepe scarf fills in the neckline. Designed by Edith Head.

P1985-437

Here's that pleated puff shoulder again. The fur ascot and pockets add a touch of class.
(But don't ask me who Arthur L. Mc Shean is.)

Press caption:

FOR SPRING - this street costume worn by Marsha Hunt in Paramount's production "*Murder Goes to College*" is ideal. The suit is a two-piece affair of gray tweed. A cravat scarf of black kidskin and pockets of the same sleek fur add a novel accent. Other accessories carry out the black note.

ARTHUR L. Mc SHEAN
PRIVATE

P1985-469

Copr. 1937, Paramount Production, Inc.

_____

I was very proud of this brainchild. Suit, hat, bag and gloves were all of softest suede. Don't know how I overlooked adding "Blue Suede Shoes," too. But aren't the ones I'm wearing here contemporary?

_____

91985-516

Here you see the lacing motif at throat, waist and cuffs - it took a while to get dressed. Even the gloves were laced.

Press caption:

SELF-DESIGNED - is this chic town or country costume from Marsha Hunt's personal wardrobe for next fall. With an expert knack of looking ahead, Marsha designs her clothes one season in advance, and this soft suede ensemble is a knockout. The color is stone blue, and the laced effect at the throat and cuffs is novel. A vest of navy blue is worn under the blouse, and the gloves and bag are of the same suede as the outfit.

P1985-488

Copr. 1937, Paramount Production, Inc.

Capes weren't commonplace then:
Nor same fabric ascots;
Nor that use of pleats;
Nor pockets dropping below jacket level. No wonder
Mainbocher was so famous.

Press caption:

HOLLYWOOD AND PARIS - unite in dressing pretty Marsha Hunt for a smart fall fashion parade. Making her picture debut in Paramount's *"The Virginia Judge,"* Miss Hunt takes time out to model Mainbocher's stunning green and white tweed ensemble in five pieces. Robert Galer of Hollywood has designed the chamois colored felt hat, which is bound with yarn and banded in green grosgrain. The French Bootier, also in Hollywood, offers a new and smarter version of the laced oxford in suede and patent leather.

P1985-55

*The last of the Suit Section from the last year of the '30s:
Dolly Tree and her superb tailors added to my joys in
moving to MGM in 1939 for "These Glamour Girls."
The long page boy bob was new, and catching on.*

Press caption:

Dolly Tree designed this precisely tailored wool suit, its moss green skirt topped by a yellow and moss green jacket edged in black silk braid. The felt hat is of matching green with a yellow cord.

More Edith Head magic for "College Holiday." We were prodigal then with furs. The term endangered hadn't yet been heard.

Press caption:

ADVANCE FASHIONS - for spring include this charming gray kasha costume Marsha Hunt is wearing in *"College Holiday,"* a Paramount production. It was designed by Edith Head and has an interesting new bodice with a silver zipper. Platinum fox is placed in wide reveres from shoulder to waistline, and under the gray kid belt, peplums of the same fur may be worn or not, as one prefers. These fur peplums have deep, invisible pockets. Gray accessories complete the costume.

Photo by William Walling

First you saw peplums, now you don't! That visible zipper was an innovation. And that hat would flatter anyone.

In the '30s, we believed in lapels that were <u>lapels.</u>

P1985-

Copr. 1936, Paramount Production, Inc.

A trim little ensemble, this navy crepe, with its pretty white organdy blouse. Luckily, the cuffs and collar/dickey detached when soiled, for gentle hand laundering.

Edith Head had me pretty well laced up in this rose red linen dress, crisp as anything, with its cuffs and collar of white linen, the lacings and belt frog of white cord. I wore it in Paramount's "College Holiday."

43

Here's a brown and white-dotted summer sheer, trimmed with white pique collar, dickey and cuffs, and worn over a brown taffeta slip. When you wear taffeta, the whole world hears you approach - it rustles.

It helps to be thin, to wear horizontal stripes. A simple but striking dress in navy and beige.

*My debut at MGM came in '39 with "These Glamour Girls,"
and Dolly Tree designed stunning collegiate weekend clothes
for all the girls.*

*Here we all are in miniature.
Left to right:
M.H., Tom Brown,
Ann Rutherford, Owen Davis Jr.,
Mary Beth Hughes, Lew Ayres,
Lana Turner, Peter Lind Hayes,
Anita Louise, Richard Carlson
and Jane Bryan.*

Press caption:

BRIGHT BLUE WITH PERSIMMON TRIM - fashions Marsha Hunt's sport ensemble, which she wears in Metro-Goldwyn-Mayer's *These Glamour Girls.* The one-piece dress, designed by Dolly Tree, is in a silk jersey, buttoned in gold. With it the actress wears a bellboy hat in blue flannel, with silk braid in persimmon caught at the side with matching gold button. A bright persimmon ascot is tucked into the neckline, with navy and white shoes and slip-on gloves.

This was a pet go-to-lunch outfit of mine. I might have worn it to the popular Vendome on Sunset Blvd. to meet the fiancé of a chum in New York, who asked me to give the fledgling actor some comfort and advice. His name was Zachary Scott. He needed neither for long.

Press caption:

COME HITHER HATS - are the rage in Hollywood this summer. Marsha Hunt, Paramount player, chooses this black straw model, banded in grosgrain and veiled in gossamer silk thread as a finishing touch to a flower print with a black background. A choker of lemon yellow beads worn outside the draped, high neckline, and the surplice sash on the printed dress carry out a soft, feminine note, which is popular in Hollywood this season.

49

Ruffles have returned, thank goodness, stressing femininity. But when we ruffled in the '30s, we didn't mess around. We show you double rows of them, no less! And don't miss the tiny fluting down the front and around the hem.

Pretty style - if you have time for all those buttons. Might be a thought for today's mother of the bride, so she needn't dress all in lace from stem to stern. And nice to wear on later occasions.

A nice summer casual in blue and white cotton print, which trims pockets, collar and cuffs of short-sleeved jacket, but the excitement is over those navy and white shoes!

A good patio lounger, this, with its split skirt, bold plaid and boldest ever white frog fasteners. Slip-on sandals with platforms were eye-catching, too.

Oh, I'd rent the skates for a picture all right, but you'd never get me to put them on - sheer terror. Gauntlet gloves and the wide sash dressed up the costume.

I was just as courageous a skier. Seeing isn't necessarily believing. And no, we didn't repair to Sun Valley or Aspen, but instead, to downtown Los Angeles, to an ice company, which had rigged up "snow" and a wintry background. It was 20° below.

How's a zippered jumpsuit, for a contemporary look? But in 1937 we called it a pajama. In polka-dotted navy satin, it made a festive at-home.

You just know there's a story to this: Remember my objections to posing for "leg art"? See Introduction. There came a scene in Paramount's "College Holiday" involving an underwater kiss with Leif Ericson and me. Had to do it, and every photographer in Hollywood rallied 'round to capture the unveiling for posterity.
This shot was taken from the ceiling, as we posed on the floor. We were matching a popular billboard ad for Jantzen swimsuits. The underwater look was added later.

I doubt that this indoor phoney fishing scene fooled anyone, but Art Director Johnny Engstead bent my pole off-scene, I struck a straining pose, and at least wore the proper fishing clothes. Now there's a <u>hat</u>!

Once I traded that hat for helmet and goggles, the same outfit served for a flying spree with Bob Cummings in his private plane, "Spinach." Yes, even then he was a healthfood addict.

58

P1726-31

Dashing Ray Milland and I, natty as can be, cross the square of UCLA's campus. And now you look at it, men's clothing hasn't changed that much in half a century.

I wore this simple gray wool suit and its handsome companion coat (next page) just about threadbare. And loved the little-girl hat, a black off-the-face beret, with green ribbons down the back. That meant a green suede belt and purse and black pumps.

P1985-517

Patch pockets, hidden buttons and long pleats distinguished this coat which could - and did - go everywhere.

56-94

I designed my red fox duo, consisting of a bolero-length jacket, which I often wore alone, and a skirt sus-pended by a wide waistband of matching copper silk braid. Caused quite a stir wherever I wore them.

I also designed my black caracul fitted coat, with its puffed shoulders and high snuggly collar, which came in handy on a Paramount junket in windy Buffalo, NY.

Copr. 1937, Paramount Production, Inc.

Persian lamb, like mink, spelled wealth, but carried an aura of quieter good taste. It was mostly worn by older women, since mostly older women could afford it.

We don't hear much about galyak these days (from lamb or kid pelts), but it was part of a wide choice of furs in the '30s and '40s. I wore my "swagger coat" of it to the Santa Anita Race Track.

P1985 574

Really, Marsha! - White spectator pumps with a fur coat? Well, at least it's <u>summer</u> ermine.

Well-cut speckled tweed, topped by snugly soft wolf collar, made a handsome coat.

My pride and joy, this superb black wool evening coat, with its leg o'mutton sleeves and even a slight train, and a portrait ermine cape/collar. We passed it around the family for great occasions, and I have it still.

Talk about clothes with lines, here is Exhibit A. You can't beat black velvet with white lace.

Here are three views of a dinner ensemble I designed and had made at 17, while still living in New York City. Gray wool tweed fitted jacket over a dress of the same. And even same-fabric sandals, custom-made, costing about $12.00. I miss those days!

70

Ever anxious to cover my long neck, I craftily devised an ascot of coral velvet, which fanned out to tuck into the square neckline of the gown. The coral chiffon velvet also narrowly banded the extended shoulders.

And here, the surprise, seen only from behind: a back, bare to the waist, above a few coral velvet buttons, below which is cascaded flouncing. When I wore the jacket, the whole effect was vaguely like a period riding habit.

Wearing this out dancing one night, I spied a woman sketching it on her tablecloth! The waiter later told me she paid for the tablecloth and took it away with her. I don't think I've ever felt more flattered.

71

More an elaborate hostess gown (that never would go near the kitchen) than a go-out-in-the-world formal, this sheer confection of multifloral colors, train and all, enhanced a simple gown of palest green.

Copr. 1936, Paramount Production, Inc.

Two views here of a lovely dinner ensemble designed by Viola Dimmitta. Topping it is a leg o'mutton-sleeved and fitted black crepe jacket, entirely covered by handsewn scrollwork of silk braid. Should be an heirloom, but it wasn't mine.

Beneath the jacket, the satin coin dots give interest to the sweet and discreet bodice. If you're slim, there's nothing like a high-waisted skirt to make your shoulders look broader. But if you happen to be hippy, look out below!.

I loved turquoise blue, I loved the sleeves, I loved the way hidden horsehair bands made the full skirt billow out when whirling on a dancefloor. Note how I had used a necklace to finagle a higher collar.

Soulful, that's what, in such a heavenly float. It's Edith Head decking me out for Paramount's "College Holiday." Rib-hugging shell pink, as I recall.

White pleated chiffon gown and cape, with an emerald green chiffon sash, the first evening gown I purchased in L.A., and it took me to a lot of parties.

Overall pleats, so fine that you'd hardly call them that. And how prettily they ripple out, at the edge of the peplum. A handsome, easy, timeless gown.

Diagonal stripes and piping-edged lapels and cuffs made this an eye-catcher. But would I look so smug if, on a dance floor, I had to step backward onto the train, and sprawled all over it?

This dream by Edith Head, a perfect pouf of a portrait gown, of white organdy, ruffled and appliquéd with inspiration. I think it's what I wore in "College Holiday," dancing with Leif Ericson and singing to each other "The Sweetheart Waltz." (what else?)

But dreamy or not, you couldn't live alone and get dressed in this. Just count all those buttons! And once again, that high-banded waistline. I'm beginning to see a pattern here that I hadn't realized.

This was my own gown, and saw a lot of action on the dance floors. To help the full skirt billow, those sheer bands . . . . were horsehair! (1937 was pre-nylon.)

Of daffodil tulle, starred with gold sequins on skirt and waistband. This cloud of glamour from "College Holiday" was what Edith Head decided I should take to Washington for President Roosevelt's Birthday Ball. This gown and I appeared at seven packed hotel ballrooms, three theatres, and the White House.

Can this be the same girl? Seems to be, but at a new studio and playing a new kind of role, moving from the romantic to the dramatic, and dressed accordingly by MGM designer Dolly Tree. It's slinky and sophisticated, this green jersey bodice above multi-colored stripes. The great gold heart of a purse announces that I'm ready for love.

Here we see a rear view of all those stripes gone diagonal. And once again, as at Paramount, I'm given a high and wide waistband. We see how the jersey scarf that drapes across the neck in front simply drops casually over those sharply squared shoulders in back. The film's title is "These Glamour Girls."

*In a scene from that film, all becomingly done up by designer Dolly Tree,
are, left to right:
Jane Bryan, Ann Rutherford, Anita Louise and I, sharing a serious moment with Richard Carlson (L) and Lew Ayres (R).
Did you ever see such a skirt at a real-life college prom as Anita's? But
isn't the make-believe of movies wonderful?*

Seeing is believing. In 1936, Bob Cummings and I stroll before a Hollywood Blvd. shoe store holding a sale, with prices of $3.47 and $2.47 a pair!

Best Feet Forward

in the Thirties and Forties

P1985-484

Ah, the ways we were shod! Shoes became more varied and prettier than they had ever been. Pumps were the most popular, but we also had sandals (from beachwear to formal), oxfords (from saddle shoes to dainty high-heeled ones), Mary Janes, moccasins, ghillies, espadrilles, moderate platform soles and wedgies. Ankle strap shoes swept into popularity toward the end of the '30s and reigned through the '40s. The sling pump had a great vogue, a pump with its heel, and maybe its toe, cut out, and with just a strap over the back of the heel to keep it on. This brought great relief from toes being crammed inside the usual closed boxing of a shoe, and the nearnakedness of the heel added to glamour. But alas, that heel strap made for bumps and grooves on women's heels that we were years overcoming. Just as several decades later, the sharply pointed toe made cripples of us all.

Boots for streetwear were unknown, reserved for hardy wear in the wilds. Except in the early '40s, for a brief, high-style vogue for high-heeled, dainty boots just ankle-high. I had a friend in Hollywood, Ginny Brown, who custom-made them to molds of her clients' feet, all by hand, painting and scrollworking them in tiny cords of silver or gold on pastel suedes of every hue. They were gorgeous and flattering. I remember Margaret Sullavan delightedly wearing several pairs.

In rainy weather, rubbers were put on over shoes, sometimes with their own hollow heels to cover your shoes' heels, or like the sling-pump, with only a strap to slip behind your heel. Downpours and snowfalls were braved in galoshes, heavy rubber, wool or canvas boots that latched closed over long tongues, with many clasps. They often were flannel or fleece lined for warmth and had heavy, ridged rubber soles and heels. But now that I think of it, we did see some draw-on boots without lacings or clasps, calf-high, usually of rubber and sometimes sporting a cuff of fur or fleece around the tops.

For daytime and walking comfort, there were flat and 1-inch heels, and the Cuban, medium-height heels, about 2 inches. There was the stacked heel, looking like layers of varnished wood, its back curved but its front straight, usually 3 inches high, to support pumps and oxfords by day, and especially the "spectator" pump, white calf, usually, with contrasting leather at toe and heel, black, navy, tan, even red, often perforated and edged in tiny scallops. Dressy shoes had 3 to 4 inch heels and grew more and more naked looking, with mere wisps of straps to hold them on the foot. Of course, the higher the heel, the smaller the foot looked, and the more of bare or stockinged foot that showed, the sexier. The tip of the toe then was generally rounded, and the vamp, the length of shoe covering the toes, generally short. The look was total flattery.

Shoes came in every material, it seemed: calf, patent leather, suede, alligator and lizard skin, buckskin, pigskin, canvas and velvet. Evening slippers might be of satin, peau de soie or moiré, often dyed to match one's gown exactly, free of charge, or gold or silver kid. A new man-made miracle made Cinderella fantasies come true with "glass slippers" of a colorless transparent early vinyl that looked like no shoe at all. Toes were often trimmed with bows, buckles or beaded designs.

We could and did put almost anything on our feet. Most women could afford a varied wardrobe of shoes, and some, a pair for every outfit. Just to bring a tear to the eye, may I remind that many popular shoe chain stores averaged wares costing $6 to $8, and that the prestige shoe shops seldom set you back more than $15 to $20 a pair. In many cases, with precisely the same styles and materials, they are now being trumpeted at $50 to many hundreds per. To match an evening ensemble I had designed (page 70), I ordered sandals made up in the same gray wool. Custom shoeing indeed, which, as I recall, lightened my wallet by about $12. As a prime example of today's inflated price of necessities, I submit the cost of shoes. Let's not even discuss handbags! At this writing, the dread pointed toe, to me, at least, has returned and monopolized the market. Just try to find a foot-shaped shoe today; all you'll find are those sharply pointed weapons to put on your feet. But not these feet. I'll wear out all the shoes I now have first. And by then the terrible toes may be gone. ❦

Purses, Handbags and Pocketbooks

Since I've never been a writer of advertising copy, it's a bit hard for me to wax lyrical about purses, handbags or pocketbooks. I understand that each denote quite different shapes, though not according to my dictionary. Superior salesladies lately have undertaken to instruct me in their separate meanings, which I don't seem able to retain. To me, they're still synonyms, and since "purse" is the shortest word, I use that one the most often, probably in error. As long as I'm touching on hats and shoes in this opus, it would be unfair to leave out purses, handbags and pocketbooks.

There doesn't seem to be a whole lot to say about those in use during the period we're recalling, except that they served their purpose well, and I can't remember having a single complaint about them. I do seem to picture them as a little flatter, and lower, during the '30s than in the '40s, when women began to demand more roominess to hold more items, as the war picked up our lives in tempo and complexity. Their shape-range was about the same as now: pouches, envelopes and boxes.

In those dear, departed days when things were made to last, so were purses. They were extremely well made and usually of the finest materials. Leather was by far the chief one, and in all forms: calf, buckskin, pigskin, suede and the costly, softest antelope or doeskin. They came in every shade imaginable. Reptiles were coveted and expensive as in shoe-use. Alligator and lizard could run as high as $20. There was lots of shiny patent leather, mostly black, sometimes navy or brown. Sturdy fabrics were also used such as canvas, corduroy and velveteen.

Dressy purses came in many fabrics: satin, moiré, taffeta, faille, peau de soie, lace, eyelet cotton, velvet, brocade and the ultimate finery, petit-point. Evening purses often were beaded through out, perhaps with seed pearls, or with bugle beads, some with bead tracery of the most delicate designs. Of course, there was gold or silver kid. Clasps themselves could look like works of art.

Plastic, remember, hadn't yet come down the pike. Unless "imitation leather," which was not made to last, was an early form of plastic. The very cheap purses seemed to be made of little more than covered cardboard, and lasted about as long as the meager cash they carried about.

In my happy position as a comfortably salaried young actress, I indulged my love of clothes to include accessories. I collected a rainbow range of purses. As with shoes, changing them daily meant that none of them had heavy use for long, and thus they lasted for years in good condition. Being a squirrel, I tend to save things long past their prime time, "just in case." Sure enough, when wine returned recently as a popular color, not having been seen for decades, I bethought myself of a particularly handsome purse of wine leather, splurged on at I. Magnin sometime around 1940. A little digging turned it up, looking good as new. Probably it had cost me about $15, and there's no need to tell you what it would cost today! I carried it perhaps ten times during its reincarnation, always hearing it complimented, until one day one of its leather handles simply came apart, the leather totally dried out. I gave it a decent burial, with regret but not reproach. Time, not use, had simply caught up with it.

Purses then were beautifully lined in softest leather, suede, grosgrain or satin. And they all seemed to come with change purses, combs and mirrors. Now such niceties will cost you.

I can't recall seeing shoulder bags before the '40s. Once they appeared, they really caught on, and especially with me. A working girl most of the 6-day week in those days, each predawn would see me struggling to carry all my paraphernalia for the day ahead, from house to car and from car to studio sound stage. I always did my own make-up at home, but lugged the make-up box back and forth each day, for touch-ups as needed. Then there was the film's script, perhaps a book to read during free moments, photographs to sign, letters to answer, knitting, perhaps a batch of cookies my housekeeper had baked to treat the crew, and, oh yes, a purse! But the advent of the shoulder bag simplified things for me. I bought the largest ones available, and crammed all the trappings I could into them. This worked fine, but for the side effect. The shoulder strap supporting such weighty contents finally wore a groove in my shoulder, which was none too upholstered to start with, and so I had to give up the style or lighten its load. Neither was easy. ❧

Styles on Wheels

As if to signify our progress in clambering out of the Depression doldrums, the automobile industry presented America with several truly "spiffy" numbers around the mid-1930s. My vintage picture file can show you a couple of prime examples, which seem appropriate to include in a book on "Styles of the Thirties."

Let's not even mention their selling price at the time - can't have you weeping all over these pages! ❦

Copr. 1935, Paramount Production, Inc

1571—2/2

In 1935, during production of my first picture, "The Virginia Judge," leading man Johnny Downs and I wave jubilantly from a Supercharged Auburn 851, a great pawing-at-the-ground beast, straining to be let out on the highways, to the mortification of all lesser vehicles.

89

Next, Cecil B. DeMille's magnificent new Cord phaeton, with perhaps the sleekest lines of any car, ever. The year: 1936. Displaying it in front of the De Mille Bungalow - his properly royal redoubt on Paramount's lot - C.B. can't hide his pride in it. And yes, I was treated to a short ride.

So much for splendor. To bring us back to earth, I'm including a more attainable runabout, a 1935 Ford V-8 convertible coupe, with its own dressy touches such as slanted wheel spokes and white sidewall tires, and the racy down-curving white stripe sharply contrasting against its black body. Bob Cummings and I drove it along the Pacific coastline past a striking tree in "Hollywood Boulevard."

"Paramount's Lucky Seven"

Any bunch of girls out for a stroll? - Wrong.
"Paramount's Lucky Seven," the publicity boys dubbed us. All newly
signed to contracts in 1935, only two of us stayed more than a few years.
Left to right: Betty Burgess, Olympe Bradna, Eleanor Whitney,
Rosalind Keith, Betty Jane Rhodes, Frances Farmer and M.H.

Here we are in evening regalia. I'm wearing my own creation, daffodil yellow chiffon ruffles from head to toe, but with a surprise bare back.

L-R: *Betty Burgess, Olympe Bradna, Eleanor Whitney, Rosalind Keith, Betty Jane Rhodes, M.H., Frances Farmer.*

Can you pick which of us was (a) a singer, (b) the daughter of a circus family, (c) the actress plagued by troubles and tragedy, (d) the world's fastest tap dancer, and (e) the gal who married the manager/owner of the Beverly Hills Hotel?

a. Betty Jane Rhodes
b. Olympe Bradna
c. Frances Farmer
d. Eleanor Whitney
e. Rosalind Keith

(I'm sorry I never learned anything about Betty Burgess, to which I could refer.)

Examining the Showcase

If this collection provides a study of clothes being worn during a certain period, and that's the intent, then it's only right to examine also their showcase, in this case, me. (Helped along by other actresses in scenes from films.)

Height: 5 feet, 6 and 3/4 inches. I had been a short model for fashions in New York, but suddenly I was a tall actress for films. There were a few about as tall: Greta Garbo, Katharine Hepburn, Kay Francis, Rosalind Russell, Myrna Loy, but the great majority were shorter, ranging from 5 feet to 5 feet 5-inches. No more. Since the '30s, we've grown a long way upward. But then, the well-established tradition from silent movies still held, calling for a tiny heroine, her lovely head thrown way back to gaze up into the eyes of her towering hero, and having to stand tippy-toe to reward him with the fade-out kiss. I didn't fit the bill. And not helping the problem was a plethora of leading men of average and even short stature. I drew more than my share of them. Working in New York, I had stretched myself to stand as tall as possible. At work in Hollywood, I stood with at least one knee bent, finding ways to curl up or lounge against doorways, anything to bring me down an inch or two. Love scenes invariably found me in stocking feet below camera range, to be rid of high heels, with my hero often as not mounted on a box.

Weight: 110. While calorie counting and diet formulas haunted most women in movies, I faced the opposite problem, trying always to gain weight. Wolfing down hot fudge sundaes, rich malteds and such in the studio commissary inevitably brought snarls of envious rage, as better-endowed actresses passed my table. Greer Garson, whose figure was perfection, used to wail, "Would you look? She can even wear quilted clothes to work!"

The screen is said to add about ten pounds to all the people shown there, but I never felt it did me that favor. My legs were all right, but I never showed them. My face at 17 still had enough puppy fat to suggest a normal-weight person below it, under the clothes, provided I hid that long, long thin neck. So my collars were high whenever I could manage it. My arms, though not bony, were pretty thin, and so I was happier in long sleeves. My torso, although broad-shouldered, was small-busted and narrow around the ribs, which could make my hips seem wide, particularly with a tiny waist. I looked best in full, loose bodices, with snugly-fitted waists and skirts, or so I thought, but several designers liked to give me a high, wide waistband, as you'll find in many of these pictures. All these devices, used to compensate for my particular figure problems, added up to distinctive touches, and I became known for them.

I was blessed - I guess - with a curly profile. It certainly didn't seem a blessing to me or to the photograph retouchers at Paramount, who at first carefully straightened my nose on every still picture and then just gave up. For years my mother worried aloud that perhaps I had better have some sort of nose surgery, "to look more like other people." But

that was just the point. The problem with a perfect beauty is that people often can't recognize her. There simply is no distinguishing characteristic. It's those deviations from the perfect norm that help others identify us, and we should all be grateful for them. I remember a young actress named June Lang, a vision to behold, but each time I saw her, I had to ask who she was. No such problem for me! Besides a rounded forehead, almost no nose bridge and a nose that curved upward, even my lips curled up at the corners. Ronald Colman and his wife Benita told me they used to describe me to each other as "Curly Lips." I decided that anything that helped two people I adored take notice of me would no longer keep me awake nights.

As a model, I had always applied my own make-up. For my screen test at Paramount I was sent to the Make-Up Department, inwardly thrilled to be in the hands of the very experts who prepared so many famous faces for work each day. But when they finished, what I saw in the mirror left me stunned. I had never seen her before and wasn't sure I wanted to see her ever again. My eyebrows had been plucked away and reshaped into narrow arcs, changing my whole expression; my lashes were overlaid with strips of long, false ones, making me feel droopy-lidded; eye shadow applied immediately above the eyes, white liner was drawn between eyes and lower lashes; my nose had a lightening line down its center to make it look chiseled and narrower, and my lipstick rounded the cupid's bow, extending above the natural line. They simply had given me all the make-up touches that were then in vogue. With no delusions of being a beauty, I just felt altered, rather than enhanced. I comforted myself that surely it would photograph better than that. But when finally I saw my screen test, there was that strange girl again, looking very odd, at least to me. I'll never know why they signed me, looking like that. I vowed then, always to do my own make-up thereafter, and with the exception of old-age roles, always did. I had heard that Garbo made herself up, and used that argument to help my rebellion succeed. Actually, the studio was nice about it. Besides, Paramount's heavy production schedule kept the Make-Up Department hard-pressed to turn out all the needed faces on time. One less helped. And at other studios, they simply accepted my custom, putting me down as an eccentric.

To me, deep-set eyes are the loveliest and most expressive. I was not so blessed. Instead, my teenage eyelids puffed a little, with no visible crease defining the top of the eyeball. As a model, fussing and fuming over those upper lids, I had devised an eye make-up that helped nature along a bit.

The prevailing custom of wearing eye shadow right above the upper lashes, seemed wrong to me, making the eyes look smaller and obviously made-up. Instead, I left that lower part of the upper eyelid, the part that blinks, (Let's call it the "blinker") its natural color; then drew a strong line with eyebrow pencil along the groove that separates it from the upper part, (Let's call that the "brow mound") and shaded it out upward, clear to the eyebrow. Then, if I lifted my brows the slightest bit, not enough to go around looking surprised, behold! I had deep-set eyes.

The interesting thing was that the effect didn't look like make-up. Studying light source, I found it nearly always came from above (sun, sky, overhead fixtures and principal lighting for photography). Ideally, brow mounds would slope below the brow, back and inward to the crease, and curving away from overhead light, would be in shadow. The "blinker," emerging from the crease right down to the lashes, would curve outward and therefore catch light from above. I simply applied

Copr. 1936, Paramount Production, Inc.

96

shading to create that effect. It was make-up hocus-pocus, but carefully applied, it looked natural and certainly worked for me. Studying stars' portraits, I was delighted to discover that Garbo used exactly that technique, in her case to emphasize her already very deep-set eyes. I was in excellent company, with my rebellion from custom. That has been the main key to my make-up over the years, and gradually, as I matured, my eyelids actually took on the contours I

wanted, which can only be mind over matter.

I never used blue or green shading. Both seemed to me to compete with eyes of those colors. Rather, I used pencils the color of my brows, brown, and sometimes gray or taupe, or a blend of the two.

If all the above seems to be in excruciating detail, I apologize. But we women spend an awful lot of time and money trying to improve our appearance, I guess we're even expected to. If this description proves helpful to anyone sharing my particular problems, I'll be glad, and the rest of our readers, I hope, indulgent.

In 62 films, I wore false lashes in only three, each time dictated by the role I was playing. My own lashes were fortunately full, so I simply mascaraed them heavily to avoid appearing too pallid and bare beside actresses who wore false ones. And I was spared a lot of bother.

Also, except for the demands of certain roles, I generally wore colorless polish on my nails, with occasional flings toward the dramatic. I'd been well-cowed by Cecil B. DeMille early on, when we were posing together for some publicity pictures at Paramount. The great man saw my flame red nails, seized my hands and held them out for the scornful inspection of the people around us, declaiming, "Look at those horrors! How can such a feminine, refined young woman go about with fingers that look as if they have been dipped in blood!"

Actresses' Appearance in Public

Clothes were a big absorption in those days. What we wore in our personal lives, outside of our homes, was of great importance - part of the image of ourselves as screen personalities that we presented to the public.

The most casual errand to the market meant a careful make-up and coif, atop a well-assembled, color coordinated outfit because we were more than likely to be spotted, stared at and waylaid for a few words or an autograph. We mustn't let the ticket-buyers down by looking sloppy or even ordinary. There was a lot of upkeep to it, trying always to look one's best. But we took pride in it, and besides, it was all just part of the job, a mighty privileged job.

Sometimes it took colorful turns. I recall seeing Susan Hayward in a Studio City hardware store, dressed as for a formal garden party, in a large cartwheel "picture" hat, a ruffled flowered chiffon dress and dainty high-heeled sandals - quite a vision. Perhaps she really was headed for a garden party, and had just stopped off first to do an errand, but it was a memorable appearance, there among the pots and pans.

It was years before my husband could talk me out of the inevitable white gloves. And I gave up hats with a deep sigh. To this day, I must "clean up" or change clothes before dropping by our neighborhood drug-store or post office. The early training ran deep.

No need to point up the contrast between that philosophy and more recent ones - they've been well noted, in the sloppy, schleppy public appearances of many a box office actress, who nonetheless kept right on being box office.

We saw an actual vogue for dishevelment, which nearly all young players slavishly followed. But now actresses freely choose their own public image - messy, dressy or in between - according to each taste.

And perhaps that's a good thing. ❦

Pictures of '30s Hats

Copr. 1937, Paramount Production, Inc.

Copr. 1937, Paramount Production, Inc.

Copr. 1936, Paramount Production, Inc.

Copr. 1936, Paramount Production, Inc.

Copr. 1937, Paramount Production, Inc.

Copr. 1937, Paramount Production, Inc.

Copr. 1936, Paramount Production, Inc.

Copr. 1936, Paramount Production, Inc.

Copr. 1937, Paramount Production, Inc.

Copr. 1937, Paramount Production, Inc.

Copr. 1937, Paramount Production, Inc.

Copr. 1935, Paramount Production, Inc.

104

Copr. 1936, Paramount Production, Inc.

Copr. 1936, Paramount Production, Inc.

105

Copr. 1936, Paramount Production, Inc.

Copr. 1936, Paramount Production, Inc.

My very favorite picture of '30s hats: 10, count them, <u>10</u> Santa Barbara ladies sporting identical tilts to their nearly identical white straw brimmed hats, and taken while shooting "Hollywood Blvd." there; Director Robert Florey front row, right.

107

"Marsha," a portrait by Edwin McQuoid, was awarded "best picture of the year" in the "Finalists" class. This print was given top honors by all four judges at its first showing and held its position through a series of exhibits.

ROTOGRAVURE SECTION - LOS ANGELES TIMES - DECEMBER 15, 1940

What Price, Personal Wardrobe?

Enjoying clothes as I did, in a continuous glare of publicity, and making enough salary to spend fairly well for my wardrobe, the choice arose: whether to splurge on a very few fine originals, or for the same money to buy a much greater variety of less expensive things. The first course would give an instant aura of success, would have snob appeal, and would set me in the heady company of the really few major stars, who usually spent fortunes on their wardrobes. The catch there was that I could afford only one or two such custom-designed originals for daytime, for cocktail/dinner wear and for formal occasions; whereas, those top-salaried stars seemed to have inexhaustible wardrobes of "creations." My family and friends, the fans and photographers all would have tired quickly of seeing me show up time after time in the all too familiar few exclusives. I'd have hated being so confined to sameness, however elegant.

I opted for quantity, for less costly variety, and shopped often and carefully among middle price range ready-made racks in department stores and a few smaller shops. One such favorite was Nancy's on Hollywood Boulevard, a block west of Vine Street. Nancy's had an inspired buyer, and I would fall in love with gobs of gowns on each shopping spree there, then agonize through the elimination process, finally heading for home, with only three, four or five things, from the dozen or more I longed for.

Nancy's had a personable manager, Paul Rose, who took real interest in my selections. The sales staff and fitters all became friends. My broad shoulders, long arms and the longest waistline in town didn't jibe in ready-made clothes, with a 22-inch waist and 35-inch hips, so nearly everything had to be altered to fit. I'd get a generous size to accommodate my upper half, liking the comfy looseness, which also disguised my thinness. Then we'd whack out the fullness at waist and hips, often to fit like skin, and to show off the narrow waist and compact derriere.

I often shopped in pairs, working in a visit with my close, dear sister Marjorie, or the lovely, gifted RKO actress Anne Shirley, or with blonde and winsome Louise Stuart, a fellow ex-model at Paramount. She taught me the value of understatement in clothing, and exemplified in her appearance, the look now referred to as "preppy" - tailored simplicity, mix-match tweeds, cashmeres, and silk separates, all suggesting casualness, good breeding and great cost.

It's odd, now I think about it, how we wanted our clothes to look expensive. Why was that, I wonder, when we had all been taught to be thrifty and careful with money, and had to be, all through the Depression? I, for instance, had been trained to turn off all lights and water faucets I wasn't actually using. (And still do.) I was given an allowance all through high school of 25¢ a week to see me through such luxuries as candy bars, ice cream and movie magazines. ("I'll get Photoplay this month if you'll get *Modern Screen;* then we can trade.")

Why then, weren't we proud of spending little on our clothes purchases? True, if a friend complimented something I was wearing, I'd be quick to admit, "and I got it on sale at Saks for only $- - - -!" The general public, though, was supposed to think it had cost a fortune.

Coming into films, I was fitted into a prescribed formula, long established by the studio publicists and gossip columnists, and one I knew well from my scrutiny of fan magazines. We were expected to be Special. Our purported egalitarian society, where we were all created equal, nonetheless required a substitute for royalty, people we could admire and envy, people of privilege who lived glamourously. And while we had society columns and pictures in the press showing us the rich at play, they seemed remote to us and weren't always pretty to look at, whereas movie stars were people you felt you knew intimately. Hadn't you watched them through all kinds of emotions? Didn't you recognize them just by the sound of their voices? And besides, they were mostly prettier and handsomer than the rich.

Thus, we headliners in films became America's royalty substitutes. Extravagance, or at least self-indulgence, was expected of us.

Thus, I kept up the pretense of being richly clad.

Furs

What I did splurge on, was furs. In Southern California? you ask. Absolutely. In justification, we do have a few really nippy nights each year, and film folk did travel a lot on publicity, location and vacation trips when the warmth of furs was appropriate. It was the mystique of furs, though, that counted on home ground, worn in movies and in our publicly private lives. They spelled luxury, glamour and sensual allure as nothing else did. I can still picture Marlene Dietrich, swathed in billows of fox furriness in . . . was it "Shanghai Express"? And more recently, can anyone who saw her forget Geraldine Chaplin at the train station in "Doctor Zhivago," delectably resembling a white fur snowball? Such screen visions didn't hurt the fur trade, local or global.

Whoever heard of a film premiere whose celebrated audience failed to make it also a fashion show of furs? Starlets who wanted to be seen at such events, but who couldn't afford to buy luxurious fur wraps, often had arrangements with local furriers to rent their needed splendor. And one of the town chuckles was about the actors' agent, very successful but also very ugly, who showed up at premiere after premiere with a succession of gorgeous young things, all in turn clad in the same full-length fox wrap. It was his own property, and he used it as bait for each date.

Over a 15-year span, I amassed: a fitted black caracul coat I designed (page 63); a boxy swagger coat of white galyak, flat lamb or kid, (pages 65 and 145); a lynx jacket (above & page 112); a 3/4-length white fox coat (page 112); a two-piece red fox coat I had designed (page 62); a black and white plaid wool coat with huge white wolf collar (page 112); a regal long black wool evening coat with a cape/collar of white ermine (page 68); a black fox muff and hat, and a cocoa beige stone marten muff (page 118) and hat, besides the mink (pages 295 - 297).

That reads today like an appalling self-indulgence, to say nothing of the carnage of lovely wild animals it represents. But in that day, wearing furs was considered appropriate for actresses in the public eye, and diminishing wildlife was totally unconsidered. We had the innocence, and the guilt, of ignorance. 🐿

Copr. 1937, Paramount Production, Inc.

*Well befurred, I attended many a movie
preview and occasional full-dress
premieres with my fiancé, Jerry Hopper.*

Fur Muffs, Cuffs, Collars and Scarves

Muffs, those fur tunnels and doughnuts in whose comforting warmth women used to encase their hands when venturing out in winter, had a revival during the '30s and '40s. They conjured up a Currier & Ives impression of delicate womanhood, braving the elements for a winter stroll, or skating over a frozen pond beside a mufflered manly companion. Certainly they were a practical item to have, in the days before heated transportation, when getting about on foot or in something pulled by horses could threaten frostbite in severe weather.

Probably the revival was prompted by such films as "Little Women" and "Anna Karenina." Motion pictures set in another time, aptly called "period pictures" in the trade, often set off fashion trends for contemporary women. Of course, the film about an earlier day had to be a box office success, one the public flocked to see, to have that influence on "the way we wore." I never heard of an obscure movie prompting a derivative fad for some article of dress. Like as not, a period big hit movie would spawn a trendy bandwagon rush for the latest oldie-made-new article, the newspaper ads featuring photos of the film's star, so garbed. We were expected to reason that if Hepburn or Garbo or De Haviland, Faye, O'Hara, etc. looked that ravishing in whatever it was, so might we, if only we wore the same thing. The tactic often worked, and off we all rushed to the stores. I've often pictured fashion designers going to see a period hit movie, hopefully armed with sketchpad and pencil, to replicate anything promising on the screen.

In any case, I loved the couple of fur muffs in my own wardrobe, and carried them in cooler weather, whenever doing so wasn't downright silly. The large, flat, rectangular stone marten, of cocoa beige to cream, went softly and beautifully with no end of daytime costumes, as did the small black fox circlet to after dark functions. Both their linings had zippers to interior purse space, which spared the need to carry a purse as well, and both had hats to match.

I also carried a muff of white ermine in "Smash-Up" to a party at Susan Hayward's, even though it was strictly an indoor event. Not meant to suggest that she didn't heat her apartment properly, it simply enhanced the all white outfit I wore. Mind you, the atmosphere was chilly enough between our two characters at that point in the story. But very soon thereafter, things heated up to the point of a rousing hair-pulling and general mess up, the sort of scene you can shoot only once. If we'd had to go for another take, it would have caused a delay of at least an hour, while my sleek coif was restored. Fortunately, Susan, a thorough "pro," gave our first take (and me!) her

Susan Hayward and I size each other up tensely in "Smash-Up," the ermine muff on my lap. Travis Banton designed our finery.

best shot, whacking, slapping and hair-pulling away like one possessed, and mercifully, Take 1 was "a print." (It's on page 380) Travis Banton dressed us for the fray.

Fur was such a studio designer's favorite enhancement of actresses' costumes that it collared, cuffed and hemmed all kinds of outfits. Quite often it would appear on the screen inappropriately. Many a workinggirl character would show up so richly fur trimmed as to prompt audience suspicion as to her poor-but-pure status. In my early leads at Paramount,

mostly playing middle to upper-middle class roles, I, too was fairly furry.

As to American women generally , once we'd climbed out of the Depression, I think most everyone could afford some kind of fur collared winter cloth coat. But fur as a trimming on suits and dresses was pretty much of a luxury, though, and limited to those who could afford fur coats as well.

In those years, a favorite touch of luxe was the wearing of a silver fox skin slung around the shoulders like a just bagged trophy, the poor creature's

My muff and I beat a discreet retreat as Susan's storm clouds gather.

paws dangling, claws and all, and its beady glass eyes gleaming, while a spring placed inside its jaws made a clamp to fasten onto its tail.

In this scene from "Carnegie Hall" Martha O'Driscoll makes a more graceful draping of her double silver fox scarf.

Just as popular were mink or sable skins, several strung together to make ends meet around Milady's neck or shoulders. The style always repelled me, and I was pleased to see it disappear sometime during the '40s, but not before, like it or not, I wore the fur piece style in "Take One False Step." ❦

Frank McHugh ushers Martha O'Driscoll and elderly me into our "Carnegie Hall" box, her silver fox scarf gracefully arranged.

Here, my character was doubtless grateful for the warmth of the skins out there in the cold, hiding on a balcony while William Powell hoped Felix Bressart wouldn't take his deep-breathing exercises outside. Designer: Orry-Kelly, 1949.

The stone marten muff gave accent to an all black outfit in a public appearance congratulating war workers on their production record.

Mink capelet and cuffs enrich my outfit as I deliver a richly deserved spanking to Douglas Scott, held down by John Howard, in "Easy to Take," even if the spanking wasn't.

In "The Human Comedy," I present my tieless new love, James Craig, to my mother, Katherine Alexander. To show how rich we are, Irene dressed her in bracelet cuffs of sable, no less.

120

Fitch, as I recall, is what so lavishly lapelled my coat in "Easy to Take," with John Howard. It's a fur we never hear about these days, (endangered?) but which my dictionary describes as the "pole-cat of Europe."

An alfresco snack with
Kent Taylor in "The
Accusing Finger," and
I'm befurred this time
with mink-edged lapels.

Copr. 1936, Paramount Production, Inc.

A white fox stand-up
collar helps me stand up to
big shots Edward Arnold
and Edward G. Robinson,
who play the title roles in
"Unholy Partners."

122

Wolf deliciously trims this coat, but who's afraid
of the big, bad wolf gorgeous Kent plays, still in
"The Accusing Finger"?

On Turning 19

A nice way to turn 19 is for your mother to throw you a surprise birthday party and invite all your leading men! Minus their wives and dates, here we are.
Clockwise:
Leif Ericson, Kent Taylor, Paul Kelly, John Howard, Johnny Downs, Buster Crabbe.
Unable to come were John Wayne and Bob Cummings.

I'm garbed in sort of a sleeveless, female tuxedo. ❧

Copr. 1936, Paramount Production, Inc.

Copr. 1936, Paramount Production, Inc.

Dogdom

Denied a dog while growing up in New York City, as soon as our family was settled in a house in Hollywood, I headed for the local dog pound to provide a canine orphan with a loving home. We named our handsome mongrel Jud, after my first film, "The Virginia Judge" And for contrast a year later, added a blue-blooded Bedlington terrier enchantress officially named Sparkle of Springdale, whom we renamed Pupchen. This lovely lady started a dynasty of Bedlingtons, loved and admired by all who knew them.

These shots record my first proud show-off visits to the Paramount lot with each. My Jud outfit is all black, the wool jacket bound in silk braid, the slit skirt narrowly striped. The blouse is shell pink pleated chiffon, with matching gloves. Jud sports a red nail-studded collar and a strong leash. Pupchen brought me out in my favorite gray wool coat, with black accessories. ❦

Copr. 1936, Paramount Production, Inc.

127

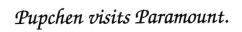

Pupchen visits Paramount.

Getting Pupchen and Plugit set for a picture.

First, the fondling.

Then, the briefing.

One down, one to go.

And finally, the pose.

WELCOME AT THE WHITE HOUSE

Frederick Jagel, M.H., Robert Taylor, Maria Gambarelli, First Lady Eleanor Roosevelt, Jean Harlow, Mitzi Green, and in the background, Capitol City Commissioner George Allen. Stoic Mrs. R. braved the cold without wraps.

Copr. 1937, Paramount Production, Inc.

FDR's Birthday Ball, 1937

President Franklin Delano Roosevelt's birthday was on January 30th. I don't know how much fuss was customary about U.S. presidents' birthdays, but FDR's 55th in 1937 was a lulu, at least for me. In his honor, 5,000 Birthday Balls were held in cities all across the country and in seven major hotel ballrooms in Washington. The proceeds from all of them went to treat victims and intensify research to combat polio (infantile paralysis) which attacked so many children and adults (300,000 in '37) and had crippled our popular president. Sums so raised over the years underwrote such medical breakthroughs as the Sabin and Salk vaccines, which virtually vanquished polio as a public health hazard. In 1938, the annual drive was given its catch name, The March of Dimes, which flourishes still, although now widened to include various birth defects. But 1937's campaign, the biggest yet, must have been The March of Dimes' genesis.

For the festivities in the capitol, Hollywood sent three emissaries. I don't know who picked them or how, but they were Jean Harlow, Robert Taylor and Marsha Hunt?! There must have been 50 or more stars then with far greater fame and box office than I had, but who was I to argue with such an invitation? And such company! What might have brought it about was the tendency of the Washington, D.C. press to refer to me as a "local girl" and "Washington's own," since my paternal grandmother, twin aunts and uncle all lived there, and I often visited them.

Also on hand for the event were Mitzi Green, former child film star, representing variety artists, Maria Gambarelli, star of ballet, and tenor Frederick Jagel of the Metropolitan Opera.

"Platinum Blonde" Jean Harlow was at the peak of her popularity as a tough-talking sex symbol, and Robert Taylor had overwhelmed female America with his romantic handsomeness. It was quite a workout, just being around them, because their presence set off public frenzy wherever we went. They were currently making a film together, "Personal Property," which had halted production - "at great cost: $100,000," so MGM said - just to free them for this junket. Jean was subdued and uncomfortable, suffering from the flu, but gamely attended the countless appearances scheduled for us over two days and nights, smiling valorously at the staring, jostling crowds. No one could dream that in five months, after a short illness, she would be dead.

There was a manly niceness about Bob Taylor, a total lack of conceit or arrogance. He'd been kept too busy in Hollywood making movies to realize the effect they had on the matrons who saw them, until this public exposure in Washington. He had suddenly become the biggest matinee idol since Rudolph Valentino. Seeing him in person, girls, matrons and dowagers en masse were reduced to sighing, swooning, shoving and shrieking. A modest, private man, all this startled and embarrassed him, but he kept his dignity and good nature throughout - the more remarkable in that he, too, had a touch of flu.

Nearby Baltimore, not to be denied, gave him an hour's motorcade which totally snarled traffic. As his open car crawled cautiously through the seething mob, one crazed fan grabbed his tie and hung on, while the car's progress so tightened the slipknot that Bob nearly strangled. Rendered voiceless and literally turning blue, he could only pound on the driver's back to stop the car and get someone to pry the fan's grip from the souvenir trophy that almost murdered her idol. He returned to Washington hoarse, shaken, and minus any buttons left on his ripped coat, but game for the next trial by fan-fire.

My mother and I arrived a day ahead of the MGM stars, our train met by the manager of the Carlton Hotel, where we were given splendid quarters. Movie "names" were very big news outside Hollywood in those days, even the nation's capitol, which turned itself inside out in welcome. Next day when Taylor and Harlow arrived, 1,000 people, mostly female, surged around them at the railroad station, over-whelming the protective police contingent in chaotic autograph fever. And later, outside the District Building, where we were presented with keys to the city, 700 more were waiting to create more flattering bedlam. So it went throughout our stay.

Yellowing clippings from the copious press cover-age given those gala few days tell me that on just the final day, we had 14 separate appearances scheduled, and made them all. The decades between have blended them into a hazy blur of being whisked all over town in limousines, our path cleared by motorcycled police with sirens wide open - the heady thrill of racing right through stoplights, with the <u>help</u> of the police! - of waving and smiling until our cheeks ached, meeting dignitaries, signing autographs in every office and corridor, stopping off at newspaper offices to chat with drama critics and columnists, posing for pictures all along the line, giving interviews at our hotel and on various radio broadcasts, and pitches for polio-fight-ing donations, and making quick changes of wardrobe for the next major event.

But a few highlights stand out clearly in memory: D.C. Commissioner George Allen, chairman of the Birthday Ball Committee, gave us visitors a splendid formal dinner on Friday evening, attended by govern-ment officials and much of the diplomatic corps, after which, close to midnight,(!) we paid a visit to Chief G-Man, FBI Director J. Edgar Hoover and his staff at the Department of Justice, which he'd kept open, just to give us a personally conducted tour of the whole Bureau, complete with weapons and clothing memen-tos of the shooting of Public Enemy #1, John Dillinger. Style note: I wore a long fitted pearl gray satin gown and Jean Harlow, a black velvet formal, deeply hemmed with white ermine which had swept along so many dusty corridors that the ermine wound up a dismal gray, and Jean told J. Edgar: "Your cleaning woman can take the day off tomorrow. I've saved her the trouble!"

Lunch at the White House loomed in our minds next day - the president's birthday - all through various morning interviews. Then there we were, gathered on the portico of the Executive Mansion, posing for pictures with First Lady Eleanor Roosevelt. That stalwart stood in the biting January cold for a quarter hour, hatless and coatless among her well bundled up guests. Not in the pictures, but also out there to greet us, were the entire Roosevelt family except for the president, assembled for his birthday celebration: James, Elliott, FDR Jr., John and their one sister, Anna, and a host of their children. They clustered around us, as delighted to meet us as we were to meet them. They were so hearty and informal that they made the great mansion seem like a family home, and they made us comfortable and welcome, especially Mrs. Roosevelt. We couldn't get over her simplicity and warmth. Once inside, she told us that the disas-trous flooding of the Ohio River, causing widespread suffering, had forced her husband to rewrite his birthday broadcast speech for that evening, prevent-ing his joining us at lunch. "He's so disappointed to miss being with you. I know he would appreciate it if you would just pop your heads in at his office upstairs and say hello. Down the hall from the top of the stairs, third door on the right." And she waved us onward and upward.

Compliment From Head G-Man

FILM COUPLE SEE HOOVER—John Trent (left), and Marsha Hunt, film "starlet" being greeted by J. Edgar Hoover at the Department of Justice. As Pilot LaVerne Browne (his real name) Trent became Hoover's favorite pilot when he flew his plane on the capture of Harry Campbell, Karpis gang member. Said Hoover to Trent: "If you're half as good an actor as you were a pilot and substitute G-man, you're a darn good actor."

Reprinted from the Washington D.C. Herald, January 31, 1937

It was one of the slowest mountings of a single flight of stairs on record. We all started out well enough, but as we neared the top, I noticed all the rest hanging back. Bob Taylor must have hitched his shoulders half a dozen times, silent witness to his nerves. The rest were clutching each other for support and asking what we should say to the President of the United States. Jean Harlow gripped the railing as a lifeline, whispering "I can't! I couldn't, not in a million years!" Her throat was dry, her knees were knocking, and she begged us to go ahead without her. After we pried her fingers loose, Bob soothed her that she wouldn't have to say a word, and we inched along the corridor to the third door, where we pulled up, a group still-life. Moments passed until, realizing the stalemate, I stepped forward and knocked on the door. The famous tenor voice called out a hearty, "Come in!" And once again, it was my hand that turned the knob and opened the door.

Where did all this boldness come from, when world-famous stars were too awed to function? I can only think it was because my parents were staunch Republicans who were apt as not to refer to FDR as "that man in the White House," and while I wasn't at all clear on what it was they objected to about him and his policies, he was surely less than a god to me. I guess I regarded him as a charismatic but quite fallible human being who held our highest office at the time.

And so it was possible for me to gaze unblinded at the familiar, beaming face behind the big desk, to advance toward him for a handshake and to introduce all of our party to him. He couldn't have been more cordial, cracking jokes to put us at ease. But the awe-spell held with the others, and our brief visit wound up more of a duologue between the two of us. I came away totally captivated and wondering about my parents' judgment.

Luncheon was served in the family dining room, with perhaps a dozen of us around a circular table, where the First Lady's sweetness and genuine interest finally routed her visitors' shyness. After lunch, she took us on a personally conducted tour of the White House. We drifted through the formal reception rooms, the Red Room, the Green Room, and was it the Gold Room? To the huge East Room for state functions, the awesome Cabinet Room, all with her breezy running commentary. We visited the impressive kitchen and met all its staff; we even inspected the linen closets. Of course what knocked us all out was the room that had been President Lincoln's - to stare at the bed where he had slept, and to hear the tale of the chambermaid in recent years who had run hysterically from the room, screaming that she had just gone in to dust it, and had seen Mr. Lincoln himself, sitting on the bed, pulling off his boots and looking "so tired, so very tired."

Listening to Mrs. Roosevelt, I found myself wondering how many times that selfless woman had led visitors on just the same house tour, and repeated the same stories that so enthralled us, just to give pleasure, and to make us all understand that it was our White House, belonging to all the American people, and merely loaned as temporary residence to each family the voters put there. It was a wrench to part from such a woman, and would have been harder if not for the certainty that we would meet several times again that evening on our rounds of the seven hotel ballrooms, and even back at the White House, to witness the President's birthday message broadcast to the nation at 11:00 that evening. It would be 13 years before I would meet Mrs. Roosevelt again and begin an acquaintance that remains an enrichment of my life.

Following an afternoon of picture-posing at all the famous Washington landmarks, and I suppose, a hasty bite of dinner somewhere, there was an early evening radio broadcast we all did on a three-station hookup. Then at 9:30, all of us dressed to kill, in our caravan of limousines, trail-blazed by those siren-wailing police motorcycles, we began weaving in and out of horrendous traffic snarls, as all Washington seemed to be hotel hopping, just as we were, from ball to ball. Each hotel's sidewalk, entrance and lobby were a crush of fans and celebrants, the crowds so dense that our uniformed stalwarts were unable to protect us as we tried to dash from car to elevator. We were clutched and patted, pulled and pushed as part of a surging mass of excited, yelling people. The District's 1,300 police, unable to control the seething city's crowds and traffic, summoned the District National Guard, the Marines and Naval Reserves to help out.

After the buffeting and pummeling we suffered, just getting in and out of the first couple of hotels, we learned caution and tried evasive tactics. Sirens were silenced as we neared each next hotel stop, and we drove around the corner from the main entrance and into a dark alley, alighting at the service entrance. No crowds there, we slipped into service elevators, slunk down back corridors, sometimes dashing through hotel kitchens before their busy staffs could notice and recognize us, and would emerge suddenly through waiters' swinging doors into the ballrooms, sawdust from the kitchen floors still clinging to our formal finery.

I'm ashamed not to recall what Jean Harlow wore that night - probably, white, to match her hair and milky skin. I'm sure both it and she were gorgeous. I wore the pale yellow confection of tulle ruffs, punctu-ated by gold sequin belt and scattered stars, from my "College Holiday" wardrobe, designed by Edith Head (page 81). It barely lasted the rigors of the night, and never recovered from its wounds.

Among the old clippings, I found a list of the orchestras playing for those balls in Washington and in major cities' Birthday Balls around the country, all broadcasting throughout the night on network radio. They provide a pretty good reminder, if incomplete, of the great big-name bands of the day: Glen Gray and The Casa Loma Orchestra, my own favorite; Guy Lombardo and his Royal Canadians; George Olsen, Ted Weems, Leo Reisman, Horace Heidt, Ben Bernie, Gus Arnheim, Hal Kemp, Benny Goodman and Ted FioRito. Ah, but those really were the days!

Alas, we were not there to dance that night. Once we were spotted, the music would stop, and following a drumroll, we'd be introduced from the stage or bandstand, where we'd each greet the crowd and compliment them for supporting the fight against polio. Then, just as the alluring dance music resumed, we'd be collected and steered through the crowds by our flying-wedge escort teams, back along the same furtive route, and off to our next port-of-call. This went on for five hotel appearances. There would be two more ahead of us to visit, besides the Capitol and Earle Theatres, well past midnight, and finally a 2-5 a.m. gala Gold Plate Breakfast Dance at the Carlton.

But just before 11:00, we were driven back to the White House - the second time in one day! - and guided to a room below the main floor, where, once inside, we were suddenly in a quite different world from the noisy bedlam we'd just left.

Behind a desk sat the President, facing a battery of microphones, lights and newsreel cameras and their operators, making last minute adjustments in their equipment. Each instruction to each other was made in hushed whispers. Ringing the room and respectfully standing were perhaps 20 silent people, aides, newsmen and the President's family. It was pretty crowded, and as I looked around for a place to stand, Jimmy Roosevelt reached out a hand and drew me over next to him, right beside the desk, just out of camera range.

The President looked up from his notes as we came in, gave us a cheery wave, and then with a wicked grin, asked us, "Is my toupé on straight?" and tugged at his own very real hair. A discreet titter rippled around the room, followed by breathless silence as the earphoned radio network men signaled only seconds to "airtime." Then one of them gave him the downward slicing pointed finger, the go-ahead, and Franklin Roosevelt began his birthday message to the nation, simultaneously carried over all three radio networks and filmed by several newsreel cameras. The President spoke of the flooded Ohio River emergency, praising those responding to it; he traced this now nationwide campaign to treat, research and ultimately prevent polio; off the air, the President asked how most of the funds raised would stay in each community to help its own victims, and thanked the public for caring and helping out. He spoke with deliberate sureness in the melodious, friendly voice that helped bring America through the Depression and WW II, just as surely as Winston Churchill's crisp eloquence later helped bring England through its wartime ordeal.

When he finished and was off the air, he asked the newsreel men if they wanted to reshoot any part of it. They replied that, no, it had been perfect the first time. Then thinking of that coveted nickname the studio film crews give to an actor who is known for getting a scene right on the very first "take," I was astonished to hear my own voice softly muttering: "One-take Frank!" Jimmy Roosevelt heard me and chuckled. Then to my horror, he sang out, "Hey, Pop! Did you hear what Miss Hunt just called you? She said you were "One-take Frank!"

A great gasp went around the room, followed by a more intense hush, as we all awaited his reaction, and I wondered to which part of the world I might be banished for my brashness. Then FDR threw that great head back and howled with laughter, followed, now that it was safe, by everyone else. And on that jolly note, we parted.

The next day, four wire services told the world's press what a funny and daring name Jean Harlow had called the President of the United States. Apparently the Paramount publicity man escorting me for the evening hadn't been able to squeeze into that crowded room, but the MGM man had. Only one Washington paper revealed the fact that the impulsive blurt had been mine. I was just glad not to be exiled. 🌿

The '30s Social Scene

Nary an Orgy

As to our gay, mad social whirl, I'm afraid I can't provide any titillating tales of naughty nightlife. Whatever such went on in those days and nights, nary an orgy or leap into a swimming pool, naked or fully clothed, did I see. My earliest range of revelry in Hollywood ran from Academy Award Banquets (that's what they were in those days), formal premieres of major movies and occasional large parties, to dinner and dancing dates at the Coconut Grove, the very "in" Trocadero nightclub (later renamed Mocambo), or at those huge dance palaces, the Palomar and the Palladium (more bourgeois, but better dancing space to better bands), movie sneak previews, birthday, beach and Ping-Pong parties, weddings and baby showers. Pretty tame stuff, but we didn't know it.

My very first Hollywood party was at Pat and Charles Boyer's home, where other guests were Irene Dunne, Ginger Rogers, Norma Shearer, Myrna Loy, Joan Crawford, Merle Oberon, Claudette Colbert, Gary Cooper, Fred MacMurray, Ray Milland, Ronald Colman, Cary Grant, Randolph Scott, and many more gods and goddesses of mine. After that 17 year-old's introduction to upper crust social Hollywood, I would never again know quite such gulping, inward tingling dazzlement; but that didn't keep me, that same night on the outdoor terrace, from trouncing both David Selznick and Irving Thalberg at Ping-Pong, and being rewarded with a dinner party invitation to the Thalberg-Shearer beach house in Santa Monica.

Most of my companions in those very first years were the younger crowd: Anita Louise and Tom Brown, Anne Shirley and John Payne, Betty Grable and Jackie Coogan (those were the going-steady pairs); and Mary Carlisle, Rochelle Hudson, Deanna Durbin, Ann Rutherford, Jane Bryan, Bonita Granville, the Bob Cummings, Jimmy Ellison and his sisters, Johnny Downs, and John Howard.

Then serious dating with a man nine years older slowed down that junior whirl and once married and starting to mature, I found also rewarding friendships with less celebrated film people such as writers, cutters, musicians and composers, and some outside the industry. Small dinner parties with lots of music at each other's homes, and lazy Sunday afternoons around friends' pools were our idea of a fine time, with occasional weekends in the snow at Lake Arrowhead or Big Bear Lake, and at the desert in Palm Springs, three of Hollywood's favorite Southern California resorts. 🐛

In 1936, New York school chum Anna Erskine (later to marry Russel Crouse, half the legendary Broadway playwriting team of Lindsay and Crouse), Gary Cooper and I pay Bing Crosby a visit on the set of "Rhythm on the Range."

At some all-Paramount festivity, 1935, front row, left to right: Ida Lupino, Kitty Carlisle, Kathleen Burke, Marina Schubert, Gertrude Michael, Carl Brisson,(don't know the man in the white tux), Bing's brother Larry Crosby, M.H. and Johnny Downs. Standing: Lynne Overman, Roscoe Karns, Buster Crabbe, Fred MacMurray, Ray Milland, Jimmy Dorsey, Jack Oakie, Joe Penner, (another mystery), Rosalind Keith, Harold Lloyd, Fred Stone and Richard Aldridge.

Same party, smaller group, front, left to right: Toby Wing,
Benny Baker, Grace Bradley, M.H.
Standing: Johnny Downs, Jack Oakie and Marina
Schubert.

Betty Smith, niece of Charlie Chaplin, was as avid a movie preview goer as were Jay and I.

My sister Marge and I were an invincible Ping-Pong doubles team, and nearly twins here, in identical white slacks outfits, but for her big red flower.

I had known and loved Glen Gray's Casa Loma Orchestra from my New York teenage dancing dates, and whenever they came to Hollywood, Jay and I were on hand to greet them.
Left to right: Glen and Vocalist Pee Wee Hunt.

As I recall this, it was a hayride party Grace Bradley gave, with our hostess starting off the seated row, then, left to right: Gail Patrick, Jackie Coogan and Betty Grable. Standing: One I can't name, M.H., Natalie Draper, Tom Brown and Rosalind Keith.

Reprinted from fan magazine

142

Helping Ann Rutherford turn 21 were, Left to right: John Payne, Bonita
Granville, a hidden mystery guest, Virginia O'Brien, Robert Stack, Anne Shirley,
Jackie Cooper, Maureen O'Hara, M.H., Patrick Nerney and Helen Parrish.

Before marrying Jerry Hopper, I was showered
with gifts at bridal shower given by Glenda
Farrell with Anne Nagle and Mary Brian.

Jay and I dine out.

The sporting life, active . . .

. . . and spectator, with Buddy Rogers at the Polo Club, before his match.

At the Santa Anita racetrack, Eleanor Whitney (world's fastest tap dancer), and I visit with Bing Crosby and a horse he's running. Alas, the horse proved less speedy at running than Eleanor at tapping.

When bosses meet: the head of Paramount Pictures, Adolph Zukor (at far end) hosts the head of New York State, Governor Herbert Lehman (near corner), in the Paramount commissary.

Clockwise from my boss: Bob Burns, director Mitch Leisen, Eugene Zukor and M.H.

Other side: production chief William Le Baron, studio exec. Henry Ginsberg, Shirley Ross, Fred MacMurray and half-hidden Mrs. Lehman.

New York's lovely First Lady, Mrs. Herbert Lehman, in
turn, has me to tea at her hotel. Her navy silk dress has trim
and hand embroidery derived from Russian peasant dress.
I'm in cherry red wool and matching toque.

147

At First, The Bride Wore...

Weddings are traditionally the most public events of most women's lives. But just because my working daily life was so very public, it seemed important to me to keep my marriage ceremony as private as possible. I've been married twice, first in the '30s and then in the '40s.

In 1938 I married Jerry Hopper, then Paramount's assistant head of the Film Editing Department, who later became a director. Jay and I drove together to Santa Barbara and were married by a justice of the peace. Before the drive, we posed for some pictures. ❧

The bride wore a wide grin and a simple, fully cut powder blue wool dress, cinched at the waist by a wide cummerbund of purple silk crepe, with a turban to match, and carried a small nosegay of violets. The groom wore a double-breasted gray flannel suit topped by a searching gaze at the future.

On these, and on pages 334 - 336, you'll have to agree that I had superb taste in bridegrooms.

Copr. 1938, Paramount Production, Inc.

Every bit as dear and gentle as he was handsome, Jay also was the funniest of storytellers. He was Assistant Head of Paramount's Music Department when we first met, before transferring to the Editing Department.

148

Following World War II, Jay's dream of directing films finally came through. He had a long and distinguished career directing many feature films and countless television shows. Though our marriage ended, we remained friends.

Ways We Wore Our Hair

During the '30s the curling-ironed "marcel," with its sharp ridges of small, tight waves, eased into softer, looser waviness, achieved now by bobby pins. You seldom saw straight hair, newly regarded as something to bend to your will - or your hairdresser's. The machine permanent wave, although an ordeal to undergo, made hairstyle maintenance a lot easier, allowing a "set" to last from one shampoo to the next.

Women generally wore their hair short, but the '20s shingle and the boyish bob virtually disappeared. Ends nearly always turned up rather than down, unless they just completed a wave. The long bob then meant hair about halfway down the neck, and its popularity grew toward the end of the decade. Hair cascading down around the shoulders, though, had to wait for Rita Hayworth and her marvelous tumbling tresses to burst on the scene around 1940. Before that, a grown woman whose hair came much below her collar was said to look cheap. All very well for Dorothy Lamour on some tropic isle, but not for mainlanders. Of course, if you were Ginger Rogers, whirling around Fred Astaire, you <u>needed</u> long hair to swing in The Swing Waltz.

Bangs weren't too popular in the '30s, but hairlines were usually masked at the temples, the cheekbones or both, by "dips." Remember Madeleine Carroll, Ruby Keeler and Madge Evans? And by the turn of the '40s, wider, loose waves were preferred, since every woman in her right mind wanted to look like Carole Lombard, or Marlene Dietrich.

During the latter '30s and throughout the '40s, hairstyles branched out in number and variety. Feminine stars on the screen provided a range of coiffure choices for the public to compare and make judgments as to which to adopt for themselves.

Ann Harding's and Norma Shearer's classic features made a tempting case for long hair, center-parted and drawn smoothly back from the face and down over the ears to form a knot at the base of the neck. But you had to be blessed with perfect bone structure symmetry and self-assurance for that trying style to be becoming, and to keep from looking like a housewife down on the farm.

Kay Francis kept her dark wavy hair center-parted and brushed back into a modified boyish bob. Her strongly defined widow's peak provided two arcs atop her forehead, a becoming frame for a lovely face. Once again, though, you had to be almost as blessed as she, to carry it off.

As to blessings, who but Greta Garbo could let straight hair just hang there beside the face, and look uniquely beautiful? Perhaps that's the hope of all the young in the '60s and '70s, with their straight-hung long curtains of hair. Garbo, however, at least kept hers out of her eyes, with bangs.

At first, Margaret Sullavan almost alone carried the banner for the pageboy bob, hers a short one, the ends of nearly straight hair barely turning under, with careless looking wisps of bangs, all giving the effect of no actual hairstyling, but rather of the becoming way her hair happened to happen. It was exactly right for the winsome actress with the foggy voice, who broke all our hearts at will. It helped the impression of a waiflike child, which she countered with a strong screen presence.

Another such exponent of the natural look was Dorothy McGuire, who startled studio hairdressers by requesting so little setting as to permit "moving hair." That was true innovation, allowing new softness and great femininity, the forerunner of all those shampoo commercials of moving hair now ruling home screens.

Constance Bennett was among the first to let big, loose waves fall slightly over one eye, producing a careless look that proved irresistibly sexy. A few years later, Veronica Lake took that cue, and wearing her long blond hair like curtains with but one tieback, managed to hide one eye completely. They named it the Peekaboo.

June Allyson looked so fetching with her baby fine hair parted way over on one side, that soon a lot of Junes were bustin' out all over.

As some hairstyles lengthened during the '40s, two styles emerged to cope with the new length. One was to fold the hair flat over itself at the back of the head, tucking ends under, with soft short curls over the forehead or over the whole top of the head, to relieve the severity. The net effect was chic and soignee. The other was a revival of the Pompadour, with forehead and temple hair brushed up and back into large smooth rolls, a Gibson Girl throwback, requiring thick hair indeed, the substitute for which was "ratting," lovely term for crinkly crepe wool inserted into the hollow hair roll, to give it body and hold. Both styles gave height over the forehead, a dimension newly discovered as becoming to nearly everyone. The rest of hair worn "Pompadour" then either hung long and loose, or also was rolled upward, making a roll ring clear around the head. The Pompadour quickly took the lead and held it, as favored hairstyle among wartime working womanhood. Once rolled and well-secured, the hair behaved itself and stayed out of their eyes, all through the long work shifts at aircraft, shipping, and munitions plants. Busy at their no-nonsense pursuits, our Rosies-the-Riveters were serene in the knowledge that their hairstyle was good enough for glamorous Rosalind Russell and Irene Dunne, among many others.

Of all the hairstyles of those days, however, the one seeming to have survived without interruption is the "feather cut." To the best of my knowledge, this was the creation of Sydney Guilaroff, chief hair stylist at MGM I am still gratefully proud that mine was the head under his dexterous hands when the style crystallized. He had already approximated it for Laraine Day. He fashioned short hair, smooth at the crown, the area covered if you were wearing a "beanie" or pillbox hat, then curling up all around it in short feathery ringlets. Curly hair or a permanent was essential to maintain it. You could be brushed into bangs, with side, center or no part, over or off the ears. It was like a softening halo around the face. The effect was so pretty and so becoming that in no time it became the prevailing hairstyle around the Metro lot. Greer Garson, Joan Crawford, Myrna Loy, Lana Turner, Lucille Ball, Kathryn Grayson, Esther Williams and more had a go at it; and I, who had changed my hairstyle with each different role, now became identified with that look.

Ever since, many women and girls around the land who adopted it have clung to it. Even today, some 50 years later, visiting retirement communities, you'll be apt to find a good portion of their distaff residents sporting still the short, soft, flattering curls of the feather cut, albeit now in varying shades of gray, white and pale blue.

Speaking of color, my impression was that outside of show business, fairly few women colored their hair during the '30s. In much of America, those who did risked being referred to as "bleached blondes" or "redheads out of a bottle." During the '40s, though, hair rinses and dyes caught on and became more respectable as the products were improved, with less margin for error, even applied at home. Permanent waving also became less torturous around that time, and friends began giving each other home perms at very little cost. Of course, all this may explain the great popularity of turbans at the same time, under which home color and/or curl disasters could hide out until remedied. In tints and dyes, the color range was widening to many more subtle and natural-looking shades.

Still, not all were subtle. Ann Sheridan, Lucille Ball and Rita Hayworth gave popularity to various shades of red. Hedy Lamarr's raven tresses reminded us how stunning black could be. And there was every possible shade of blonde. Jean Harlow's platinum white blondeness was not for everyone, but since male audiences read Harlow's message loud and clear, a number of females willingly stripped all color from their own hair in hopes of reminding their men of her.

Getting back to the feather cut and Sydney Guilaroff, one early dawn, as he was dressing my hair for the shooting day ahead, he told me that he was waging a campaign to persuade his good friend Greta Garbo to alter her accustomed long, lank lack of coif for her forthcoming film, a sophisticated comedy called "Two-Faced Woman." He was proposing that she try the feather cut. But Miss Garbo was not easy to sway. Each day for the next week or so, Sidney would report a frustrating lack of progress. Then one morning he told me she had seemed to soften, saying, "If you could just show me what you mean . . ." And a few hours later there came a call to my set, asking if I could be excused from shooting long enough to visit Miss Garbo's dressing room. To my astonishment, since I was involved in the scene being shot, production skidded to a halt, idling everyone on the soundstage. I wended my way afoot over the distance of about two long city blocks, walking with the smoothest possible glide, so as not to jar my just-combed hair - this was before the advent of hair spray - praying that no breeze would ruffle it, wanting to do Sydney proud.

When I reached Miss Garbo's door and knocked, a deep and hearty voice called out, "Come in!" and then there was the Living Legend, garbed in slacks and shirt, uncoiling from an armchair and rising to greet me. Sydney beamed and introduced us, and I held back a yelp of pain as I felt the strongest handclasp of my life, crushing my outstretched hand. She was cordial and charming, quite unlike the reputed shy introvert. But then, this was her turf and our encounter, her idea.

While I pirouetted slowly to let her see the coif from all sides, she murmured approvingly and said, "But of course, just like a Botticelli cherub!" which had not occurred to me, but she was quite right. Then we stood together, facing her full-length mirror, as she mentally tried on the style around her own perfect face. Sydney twinkled at us in the background, sensing victory.

And so it came to pass that Greta Garbo had her famous lank locks shorn and styled in a feather cut for "Two-Faced Woman," looked marvelous, of course, and never acted again! It was her last picture, and I've always harbored a gnawing suspicion that somehow, I was to blame.

Ever wonder what we did before hair spray? Here I am with Sumner Getchel on a lunch break, my hair wrapped in meline, to hold the style, so my hair in the scene we resume shooting after lunch, will match exactly how it looked before.

Pictures of '30s Hairstyles

Copr. 1935, Paramount Production, Inc.

Copr. 1935, Paramount Production, Inc.

Copr. 1935, Paramount Production, Inc.

Copr. 1937, Paramount Production, Inc.

Copr. 1937, Paramount Production, Inc.

Copr. 1937, Paramount Production, Inc.

Copr. 1936, Paramount Production, Inc.

Copr. 1936, Paramount Production, Inc.

Copr. 1936, Paramount Production, Inc.

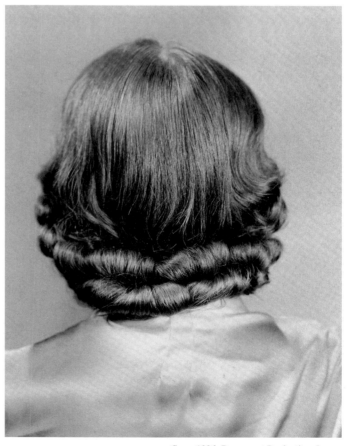

Copr. 1936, Paramount Production, Inc.

Copr. 1937, Paramount Production, Inc.

Copr. 1937, Paramount Production, Inc.

158

Metro's "These Glamour Girls" surround Lew Ayres and exhibit assorted 1939 hairstyles. Clockwise from him, we're: Jane Bryan, Anita Louise, Mary Beth Hughes, Ann Rutherford, Lana Turner and M.H.

Production Stills From '30s Films

My very first role: the romantic lead with <u>two</u> leading men, Johnny Downs (left) and Bob Cummings (right of center)! "The Virginia Judge" was Walter C. Kelly (center), vaudeville star, whose niece, named Grace, later became Her Serene Highness of Monaco. Here we are, along with legendary comedian Stepin' Fetchit (far right).

*Picture hats and organdy went
with mid-'30s dates, and here
I'm dating Johnny Downs in
"The Virginia Judge," 1935, at
Paramount in a carnival scene.*

*Flowered chiffon was another "must" on festive
occasions, and this nice lady and I conform,
along with another lacy, broad-brimmed hat.
Sorry, I can't supply her name.*

Father-daughter bitterness lingers between John Halliday and me in Paramount's "Hollywood Boulevard," 1936. If you remember that mass of straw hats (page 107), here you see me conforming to the trend.

Because Bob Cummings and I played the leads in Paramount's "Hollywood Boulevard," 1936, we were sent along that street, taking publicity pictures. Here's the timeless Chinese Theatre and its inevitable tourists. The Hotel Christie in the background is where I stayed while rehearsing my screen test, a year before. My gown is white embroidery on black net. And isn't Bob dashing?

P1985-310

Copr. 1936, Paramount Production, Inc.

164

Santa Barbara's famous Mission, Bob and I, savoring dazzling sunlight. We were there on location, shooting "Hollywood Boulevard." That film brought back such silent film favorites as Francis X. Bushman, Betty Compson, Lloyd Hamilton, Mae Marsh, Jack Mulhall, Esther Ralston and Rod La Rocque.

165

Thought you'd enjoy a behind-the-scenes peek at preparations for the pretty flower garden shot that follows. A "dolly shot," the camera will roll along the tracks. Director Bob Florey, crouches over them; cameraman Karl Streuss bends just over him.

Copr. 1936, Paramount Production, Inc.

Don't I look all alone among those flowers? Who would guess there was an army of film crew needed to get that scene? The high-up board in the other shot has gold or silver foil to catch the sun and reflect its blinding light onto the actor.

Now, how did you ever guess that this movie with John Howard was titled "Right in Your Lap?" At least, while we were shooting it. On release, it was called "Easy to Take." But why do we look so apprehensive? I've no idea.

Copr. 1936, Paramount Production, Inc.

There's wonderful old basso-voiced Eugene Pallette between John and me. Don't miss the winged collar fine old veteran Richard Carle is sporting. We really dressed for courtroom scenes then.

*It isn't just everyone who has had Jack Benny serving as a gondo-
lier. Leif Ericson and I could so boast in a scene from "College
Holiday," Paramount 1936. I'm in the gown that later went to
the White House - and me in it!*

Copr. 1936, Paramount Production, Inc.

Just checking to see if you're paying attention. You're right, this is not from a modern film, but a period one, a western Paramount called "Born to the West," now on video as "Hell Town." Don't ask me why. But since he's become a national monument, with even an Orange County Airport named after him, I thought John Wayne should show up on one page. Behold the youthful Duke of 1937.

Fine stage and screen actor Paul Kelly and I looking tense to publicize (you guessed it!) "The Accusing Finger" for Paramount. Black velvet and lace add drama.

Four good men in "The Accusing Finger": Bob Cummings, Paul Kelly, Kent Taylor and Harry Carey. But Kent, shown here, was far the handsomest, and in my mink lapels finery, I seem to be getting his message.

Copr. 1936, Paramount Production, Inc.

173

"Murder Goes to College," 1937, was kind of fun, working with two of the best character actors in the business: Roscoe Karns and Lynne Overman. Can't recall the plot, but once again, I was well-dressed.

Copr. 1937, Paramount Production, Inc.

*Apparently I'm hiding or protecting the evidence, despite
Lynne's stern demand. Can't recall who won.*

A free lance after leaving Paramount, I went to Republic Studios for
"Come On, Leathernecks!" in '38, opposite Richard Cromwell, on the right.
I'm wearing the maid of honor gown I designed for my sister's wedding.
Blue and lavender tulle, alternately layered, gave an iridescent shading.

Leon Ames is selling, but I don't think I'm buying. This suave villain in "Come On, Leathernecks!" came early in a long and distinguished career. We later played married couples in two stage plays. My tulle gown was crisscrossed over the bodice, with a scarf draped across the shoulders.

Over the side! I couldn't resist showing you how, on Republic's low budget, both the sky and the ocean were a fairly obvious stucco wall. My overboard jump into the briny deep was onto a mattress.

From Republic to Grand National to Monogram, then termed "Poverty Row" studios, which turned out feature films in six days of shooting. We wore our own clothes, except for such outfits as riding habits, which were rented. Here are Gordon Jones, Certified Check and George E. Stone in "The Long Shot."

Let us now praise (less) famous men. "The Long Shot" gathered stalwart character actors whose fine work made leads Gordon Jones and me look good. Derbyed Tom Kennedy, invariable traffic cop Edgar Dearing and jockey George E. Stone added to the calibre of countless films.

You can tell by the glitter in his eye that C. Henry Gordon plays the heavy in "The Long Shot." And for this scene I trotted out a different suit from my home wardrobe. Note it well - you'll see it again. Woven of wine and blue, the hat, purse and gloves were all blue suede, the scarf blue chiffon.

Also gracing "The Long Shot" was venerable, beloved Harry Davenport, and, as promised, here's that outfit again.

Back for a return engagement, same outfit, still Poverty Row, but a different studio: Monogram this time. I'm in the clink, (see the prison bars' shadows) and Warren Hull of radio fame gets the story. "The Star Reporter," 1938.

116-73

Here is probably how I wound up in jail, "breaking and entering," in that omnipresent suit, scarf, hat and gloves.

116-86

All dressed up to go safecracking. Even a hat, no less. Can't recall which movie. (I crack so many safes!)

Over at MGM, Lana Turner and I are starting to dress for the big prom, in 1939's "These Glamour Girls." That was Lana's very first leading role, and look what it led to!

Metro designer Dolly Tree dressed our characters differently and appropriately for our campus weekend house party in "These Glamour Girls," 1939. Left to Right: Ann Rutherford, Mary Beth Hughes, Anita Louise (having no privacy on the phone), Jane Bryan, M.H. and Lana Turner, seated.

Prom-ready: "These Glamour Girls" and their collegiate dates.
Head-to-head, from Left: Ann Rutherford/Tom Brown; Jane Bryan/Richard Carlson; Lana Turner/Lew Ayres; Anita Louise/Sumner Getchel; M.H./Peter Lind Hayes; Mary Beth Hughes/Owen Davis, Jr.

The Way We Wore

Part Two

The Forties

The Forties

The war years of the first half of the 1940s brought women's slacks into their own, proving the safest, most practical garb for the many kinds of war effort jobs millions of women undertook. Streetwear took on a more casual look as women sometimes lunched and shopped together in mix-match separates, sweater sets and skirts. Here and there the slacks suit emerged, gradually accepted as respectable at all but dressy events. The jackets that topped slacks were as carefully tailored and fitted as suits with skirts. The Eisenhower jacket became a rage, both to honor our popular General and because, reminiscent of what used to be called the lumberjacket, its short length ending at a wide waist-band, it showed off a good figure.

With broad-shoulder padding securely in place throughout the '40s, the great staple of women's wardrobes was the tailored suit once our hip width seemed to shrink, below those football shoulders. Suits were now becoming to nearly all. I think the tailored suit reached its zenith in that decade for becomingness of line and fit, for careful workmanship, attention to detail and for range of variation on a single theme.

The '40s also brought us peasant blouses and skirts, probably to give feminine balance to our infatuation with slacks. Mexican,

Russian and Gypsy derivations were seen, but especially the dirndl style of Bavaria. It had a full-gathered skirt, often in graduated horizontal sections, broken by rick rack, braid or piping of a contrasting color. It was almost always in a bright cotton print, the blouse usually white cotton, with puffed sleeves. Washably practical, they gave us the look of crisp and wholesome little girls. They covered a multitude of figure faults.

Of course we wore dresses, too, all kinds of them, and nearly always they had little hidden shoulder pads. Sleeves were often full, while draping and folds added grace and softness to the bodice. Skirts mostly hung straight and narrow, closely hugging the waist and hips. To minimize those proportions, virtually all women, even sylphs like me, wore some kind of foundation undergarment, from lace lastex pantie girdle to rigid corset.

By the '40s, the vacillating hemlines of the '30s came to rest at what I believe is the most becoming length for most women: somewhere within that inch just below the knee, and the upper calf. It permitted a good stride when wearing a straight, tight skirt, and showed a pretty curve of leg beneath a full skirt. Alas, as with all fashion, it was bound to change, too good to last. Around 1948, all the way from Paris, Monsieur Christian Dior yanked our hemlines sharply downward in what was hailed as The New Look.

Husbands took a dismayed new look at their shrinking bank balances, because since the decreed length was now a good four to six inches lower, no existing hemlines could be let out far enough to look in style. As a result, all female America went on a shopping spree for a whole new wardrobe.

At the same time, straight skirts gave way to ripplingly full ones, some flared to a full circle. And by the end of the decade, the stage was set for the Fifties Look, when ruffled petticoats made sure that Milady billowed as she walked. 🍒

Custom Costuming For Films

The wardrobe departments of the major studios had dress form dummies made for each star and featured actress under contract, shaped to her exact measurements, and on which all her costumes would be draped, shaped and fitted, prior to her arrival for in-person, on-person fittings. Those dress forms were closely guarded from prying outsiders' eyes, for there, in their muslin nakedness, and with the actresses' names clearly labeled on them, stood the unvarnished truth about the screen's goddesses: their bulges and hollows as nature had made them, before needed bust pads or waist cinchers or girdles would perform their magic; before the designe''s and fitter's art would "ac-cen-tuate the positive, eliminate the negative," until that merely human form would seem a form divine, as costumed for the screen.

Studio designers knew by heart the figure problems of all the actresses on the lot and fashioned their costumes accordingly. I for instance, have a neck often likened to a swan's. Fine, let a swan have it. I'd cheerfully have given away an inch or two of its length. Furthermore, I was so thin that my collar bones and clavicles (the bones reaching laterally from throat to shoulders) protruded. And my timing was off - Audrey Hepburn hadn't yet appeared, to display her bones as proudly as jewels. So the blessed designers helped me hide my thinness with so many inventive touches that often the necklines I wore were more original and interesting than if I'd been given the usual open collar, V-neck, or strapless formal.

At the same time, the designers cooed over my tiny waist and broad shoulders and accentuated those features. They worked this flattering magic for all of us.

A leading lady's wardrobe for an upcoming picture might call for several to a dozen costume changes. The designer's first sketches would be shown to the producer and director for approval, and suggested changes would be made before work on the clothes began. Then during the first fittings, the actress who would be wearing them could sometimes effect modifications for becomingness or suitability to the role. Of course, major stars were shown the designs first.

Once completed, the entire wardrobe would be inspected by the producer and director, the actress modelling it all for them in the largest and prettiest fitting room. This was always a crucial, tense time for the Wardrobe Department, the culmination and test of days or weeks of combined effort. As on opening night in the theatre, they now awaited the critics' verdict. You, the actress, would arrive at the appointed time, but invariably the Top Brass, the true stars of these encounters, would be late, "delayed in conference," their secretaries would report, but you always suspected they simply were staging their entrance. Sometimes you cooled your heels for hours until word was relayed from the switchboard: "They've left their office; they're starting on their way over here!"

Soon they'd wander in, jocular, feeling their power, but also vaguely ill at ease in this women's domain, invariably, their hands plunged in their pockets. One by one, you would model the costumes, standing, sitting and parading around in each, for them to see and watch it "move" as it would in the playing of its intended scene. Then the personalities of the judges would come into play. With a murmured "I don't know anything about women's clothes. If you're happy, I'm happy," they might give a blanket O.K. Or one might approve an outfit while the other one hated it, now he'd seen it worn. Then it would be argued out between them, the designer or actress playing referee and trying to sway final decision toward acceptance.

You might be treated to really relevant objections such as: "I never did like checks. My wife looks terrible in checks," or clear suggestions like: "Couldn't it have a little gizmo at the hip? It looks so plain." Generally, though, if you had your arguments at the ready, you could win out. Now and then, of course, you'd come across a man with a good clothes sense and a grasp of how well a costume can help depict a character. Just as possibly, one of them would insist on some minuscule adjustment that made no difference at all, just to feel he had made a contribution. These were revealing sessions that often told you the actress what to expect - or not to - in reasonableness later, on the set.

When final adjustments had been made, there followed the wardrobe tests shot on the set. For big "A" pictures the cameraman might shoot some film of you posing and moving about in each change. Usually, though, the still photographer would shoot you beside a chalk-marked slate identifying you and your character's name, the film, its director and in which scene number the outfit would be worn. You posed for several shots per costume: front, left and right side, and sometimes even the rear view. These often came in handy as reference for retakes, which might be needed a month or two after production, following the film's first previews, reminding you that you had worn gloves in that scene.

I often wished I could get to know the designers better. I admired them greatly and was fascinated by their skill and creativity. But they were among the hardest working people on the lot, pressed to meet deadlines, and usually had to rush from fitting to fitting. Adrian, for instance, had to produce some 500 separate designs for us hoopskirted ladies and all the elegant gentlemen in "Pride and Prejudice."

Unsung heroes and heroines are the tailors, fitters and seamstresses for the screen. Bringing ultimate expertise to their work, they perform with meticulous care and attention to the tiniest detail, knowing how close the camera may come to the subject, and how many times the big screen can magnify the slightest wrinkle or pucker. It all adds up to workmanship no Paris maison-de-la-couture could top, no matter how elaborate. The working of furs, feathers, leathers and laces, the beading and embroidering, the hand rolling of hems, all these leave the lucky wearers breathless with admiration, never looking better - and spoiled for life.

All this perfection takes time. Wardrobe people surely must retire rich from overtime pay, because their exacting work cannot be rushed. There always are absurdly close deadlines to be met, which mean stitching away, late into the night. Added hazards are directors' sudden inspirations and changes of mind as to the appropriate look for a given scene, or a last minute switch in the shooting schedule, demanding next week's costume to be ready tomorrow, or the actress not liking what she sees in the fitting room mirror. I well remember watching in stunned disbelief as a famous actress, privately nervous about an upcoming scene, literally ripped and ruined an exquisite, becoming gown, shouting salty complaints about how it made her look. She thereby got the scene she dreaded postponed as she wanted, while a new outfit for it had to be designed and made. But no one scolded her for her tantrum, and the patient wardrobe people took all the heat, and worked overtime again.

In fairness I must tell you that such offscreen histrionics are the exception, the fitters and fittee usually working with harmony and patience. And it does take patience. Some fittings of more than one costume can go for hours of standing perfectly still, and actresses have been known to faint dead away. I nearly did, more than once. While savoring the odd sensation of voices growing dim and the room seeming to go quite dark, I'd be caught as I started to sway, and kept from falling. The blood simply leaves the head, as any military, subjected to hours of dress parade in a hot sun can tell you. Those stalwarts have been known to drop like flies.

On every soundstage there was an ironing board and iron, ready if needed to remove wardrobe wrinkles just before each shot - those were pre-polyester days. You learned to sit carefully between scenes, and for a costume too elaborate or too tight to permit sitting at all, you used a "leaning board," allowing you to lie back against its slanted angle and rest your aching feet, without mussing your costume.

Usually you changed into your own clothes during lunch hour to spare the film finery and to permit you the luxury of sitting carelessly, or even spilling your food if you felt like it. Hair sprays hadn't yet arrived either, and so all over the studio commissary you'd see legendary ladies with their coifs encased in meline net turbans, that guarded against a gust of wind on the walk back to the set. (See page 153). What with those hair nets and dressing gowns or casual slacks, a studio commissary gave visitors the feeling of being backstage, and gave all of us working actors a sense of easy informality and camaraderie. It was one of the best aspects of a studio, even if the food wasn't.

Accidents to wardrobe would happen, though, during a "take" or just sitting around the set. Then you could see the wardrobe men or women in splendid action. With nerves of steel, they ignored the assistant director's apoplexy over mounting production costs of each passing minute that a set and crew were idled, and with all deliberate speed, they removed the stain or mended the rip or whatever, with stitches so

tiny you couldn't find them in a later camera close-up shot. Experts, all.

Not merely the main garment was studio-provided, but also wrap, hat, shoes, purse, gloves, scarf, jewelry and, thank heaven, hosiery. At least, so it was at Metro, where most of these recollections center. If you, the reader are old enough to recall wearing stockings of silk, rayon, lisle or cotton, until at war's end, nylon mercifully captured our legs, you remember how easily runs would appear in sheer hosiery. On a single shooting day of strenuous action, it was commonplace to go through several pairs of stockings, and it was a relief to have them all provided. Men's shirts, incidentally, nearly always were duplicated in identical spares, to keep the actor looking freshly "linened" over the long haul under those relentless hot lights. And each night, all washable items were laundered and freshly ironed for the next day's use. The nonwashables would be dry-cleaned overnight, if warranted. You might say the wardrobe departments never slept.

Shoes were mostly new, bags and gloves came either from department stores or out of "stock" - the enormous studio reserves of barely used accessories from earlier films - as did hats, unless they were designed and made especially for the new outfit. We were on our own, though, for undies. We were given only what showed. Fair enough.

If you're wondering what happened to all those lovely outfits, once the pictures were finished, don't weep for their short lives. They knew reincarnation, over and over, slightly changed and refitted for other actresses in later films. A sharp-eyed film buff spotted a bold-striped turban I wore in "Pilot #5," (see page 251 and 329) as the one Eleanor Powell had worn in a movie several years earlier. And I recall my own private tingle when I was given a quilted robe to wear in a brief scene in "Music for Millions," that had been made for Katharine Hepburn (page 372). Because of the reworkability of these custom costumes, studios rarely allowed their actresses to buy them. I did manage a couple of purchases from Universal, and treasured them.

All of this costly couture and effort was of course beyond the means of some independent filmmakers and those on "Poverty Row," those small studios turning out films with six-day shooting schedules. Those "quickie" producers often asked actors to provide their own clothes for modern stories. Or they sent a wardrobe man or woman to pick up lots of likely outfits at local department stores, then show them all to the execs and the actress at the studio, where a selection was made. The chosen clothes then were fitted to the player, and that was that. I imagine that today - except for really big-budget films - shopping for wardrobe must be the rule rather than the exception for most contemporary films being made, as it is for television shows, all but those about the very rich. They get designed.

For period costumes and western movies, then and now, the answer would be costume rental. That brings me to respectful mention of the Western Costume Company, that venerable repository on Melrose Avenue in Hollywood, home of costumes for men, women and children for just about any period or part of the world that you could name. Western Costume is where studios and independents turned for decades, (and still do, as well as to recent rivals) for existing costumes, period or modern, which could be refurbished and fitted for their pictures. I must have been costumed there for a dozen or more pictures and stage plays as well. They also execute costumes for designers lacking studio dressmaking facilities.

Back to wardrobe shopping, although it doesn't belong in a book devoted to the '30s and '40s, I'm reminded of how, in 1957, I first reported to "Wardrobe," about to make a film at Warner Brothers Studio, and was delighted to learn that my old friend from MGM days, the gifted designer Howard Shoup would be in charge of our picture, "Bombers B-52." I would be playing Natalie Wood's mother (and dyed my hair black to help a family resemblance). After our reunion hugs, "Shoupy" told me that he was swamped with designing many dozens of costumes for Ann Blyth to wear in the forthcoming "Helen Morgan Story," and that he could barely manage to costume Natalie's many changes in our film. I would need about half a dozen changes for my role. Knowing my "feel for clothes" from the early days, he asked me if I would like to costume myself. It was a great adventure, shopping alone and selecting what I thought right for my role. I even brought one or two things from home that seemed apt. They all met with Shoup's and the Top Brass' approval, but any hopes I had were dashed, of seeing the screen credits say, "Miss Hunt's wardrobe by Miss Hunt."

Designers on Films I Was In

Adrian:	1940 - *Pride and Prejudice;* 1941 - *Blossoms in the Dust*
Adele Balkan:	1959 - *Blue Denim*
Travis Banton:	1937 - *Easy Living;* 1946 - *Smash-Up.*
Edith Head:	1936 - *College Holiday*
Irene:	1942 - *The Human Comedy;* 1943 - *Lost Angel;* 1943 - *Thousands Cheer;* 1944 - *Music for Millions;* 1945 - *Valley of Decision*
Orry-Kelly:	1949 - *Take One False Step*
Max Ree:	1946 - *Carnegie Hall*
Howard Shoup:	1942 - *The Affairs of Martha;* 1942 - *Seven Sweethearts;* 1957 - *Bombers B-52*
Gile Steele:	1940 - *Pride and Prejudice;* 1940 - *Flight Command;* 1941 - *Blossoms in the Dust*
Edward Stevenson:	1940 - *Irene;* 1944 - *Bride by Mistake*
Dolly Tree:	1939 - *These Glamour Girls;* 1940 - *Flight Command;* 1940 - *The Penalty;* 1940 - *The Trial of Mary Dugan*
Theadora Van Runkle:	1971 - *Johnny Got His Gun*
Jean Louis:	1952 - *The Happy Time*

Where two designers are credited with the same motion picture, it means that a studio's head designer, overwhelmed with conflicting assignments and pressing deadlines, often delegated some of the chores to associate designers on the lot.

These are all the designers of my films that I can identify, less than half the films I was in. I've listed movies shot since the '30s and '40s as well, for whatever interest they might hold for movie buffs.

Pictures of '40s Fashions

"Kitsch": Don't think for a minute that we missed out on cutesy kitsch touches, even then. Exhibit A : A fish-net-trimmed hat, belt and purse, which also boasts two corks. Don't miss the fingerless gloves resembling star-fish. Mine not to reason why, mine but to pose and sigh!

Despite my earlier objections to posing for "leg art" photos, here I am posing, however discreetly, in a couple of poolside costumes.

A bare midriff was pretty racy in the '40s; and consider the man's shirt worn as a jacket; that fad popped up again in 1990. And don't miss those sassy sandals.

Green and white, I think, made up the color scheme of this charming ensemble, and beneath the two-tone jacket, darned if it doesn't look like another bare midriff!

202

"Tennis, anyone?" - And any time from '40s to '90s. Here's a timeless sportsdress of white cotton, the shoulders becomingly broad, the skirt's side slits allowing free movement.

203

Culottes, reappearing in 1991, and a tailored bolero jacket make a neat showing over a dark polka dot blouse.

Every woman should have a pretty quilted robe, and if the neckline is ruffled, so much the better.

Joan Crawford's shoulders were never broader than these! The pleated pants are very NOW.

Here's what we should look like when we go gardening, . . . but when did we ever? Highly romanticized, and the high, wide waistband helps you look like a "longstemmed American Beauty rose."

Here again, the raised waistline that points up a slender waist, in a starry dress of navy and pale blue, designed by Edward Stevenson for RKO's "Irene."

This simple tan street dress is made special by fine tucks in the bodice and over the hips, opening to a multi-pleated skirt. Accents are the white collar and wide leather belt.

Scrollwork embroidery across the top and sleeves distinguishes this burgundy wool dress, given added ease by the fullness at bodice and skirt. The veiled hat, bag and gloves all match.

A veil again, over a simple brimmed hat worn becomingly off the face. Such a suit should be welcome in every woman's closet. You can't top well-cut, basic simplicity.

A superb gray wool flannel coatdress, double-breasted, softened with white eyelet collar and cuffs, part of my stunning wardrobe worn in "Smash-up," 1946, designed by Travis Banton.
I loved it enough to buy it, and later wore it for this shot taken by Life magazine.
I also wore it on stage in "The Cocktail Party" until it was stolen from my dressing room in San Francisco. Months later, from a picture, a policeman recognized it as it was worn, complete with all my stolen accessories, by a transvestite strolling across Union Square.
Wardrobe envy can be a hazard.

Photos by Pell

Here's a wardrobe test, a chance to see how an assembled outfit looks and photographs. The floor slate tells the vital statistics for later reference. Side and rear views are also shot. It all helps to keep track of the sequence of costume "changes" to be worn, also hairstyles and even shoes.

These two outfits were for "Seven Sweethearts." I was fond of this one in cream and cocoa. Extra long and full sleeves, and pockets as peplums below the openwork belt made it interesting and pretty. And don't miss the pumps - but how could you?

On location in New York City, I stayed at the legendary Hampshire House, then famous for the distinctive interiors by Dorothy Draper: white accents against deep green walls. We shot these fashion stills in my suite. The dresses were quite simple, counting on accessories for accent. The pearl gray felt hat (my own) had silk scarves of royal blue and emerald green, to tie or drape as you liked. And pipe the anklestrap shoes!

214

MARSHA PICKS THESE THREE

Marsha Hunt, in RKO Radio's current vehicle, "Bride By Mistake," wears three gowns which express the uncluttered lines so popular this year. A print suit (left) is accented by matching bowed blouse, purse and shoes. Note the modified derby of crocheted straw. The two piece dress (center) features beaded tassels at the belt and tie-ends, an urban touch as saucy as it is feminine. On the right is one of her favorite dinner gowns; a light bodice criss-crossed with a design of beads repeating the dark note of the skirt. It features the square arm holes and tight sleeves, characteristic of this year's designs.

Three of my costumes for "Take One False Step" at Universal-International, in 1949, designed by Orry-Kelly.

Find a suit that suits you?

From my own wardrobe, shades of beige, tan and green blend nicely in the jacket worn over a simple beige dress. Tan straw hat, with green suede purse and pumps.

Also my own, an interesting suit of tiny navy and white checks, with white collar and white piping edging the pockets. Navy buttons descend the long double-breasted jacket, over a skirt of wide pleats. Navy and white straw hat, red and white purse and pumps completed the ensemble.

If memory serves, this crisp suit was designed in 1940 by Edward Stevenson for RKO's "Irene." The creamy white wool jacket had unusual pagoda-like lapel and pocket trim of the same black wool as the skirt.

I thought you should see one bolero length jacket, and so here's a suit of mine, the bolero of yellow and gray wool plaid, the skirt gray wool. Nice diagonal flaps, a yellow blouse and turban add to a sunny look.

This was my outfit for the windup scene of Saroyan's "The Human Comedy," when I rode slowly with James Craig in an open car, passing ethnic groups, praising and loving the diversity of America. Simple and simply stunning, MGM's Irene designed it in 1942.

Designer Irene"s magic again, this time for "Music for Millions" at Metro, 1944. Gray and black wool suit, the jacket abbreviated, closely fitted, and belted in back. The felt Tam o' Shanter hat is a matching gray.

For "Lost Angel," around '43, Irene was at her Irenest, creating suits of superb chic and tailoring. Of taupe wool, only the torso white-striped, even the hat was a custom part of the costume (page326).

MGM PHOTO By Clarence Bull

The short, boxy coat was to go casually over the shoulders as shown, or properly donned. Even the white blouse beneath shows originality with its pleats.

MGM PHOTO By Clarence Bull

Still by Irene, still for "Lost Angel," and this time navy and white, again with a short, fitted jacket, skirt and jacket distinguished by some beautifully executed fagoting, now a virtually lost art. Notice a repeat of the hat design.

226

You're thinking that acting can age a girl, and you're right! Playing my fourth elderly role before I was 30, here I am in the closing scenes of "Carnegie Hall," appropriately wearing a Hattie Carnegie ensemble in cocoa and black wool, and a wool lace-veiled hat by John Fredericks. Both were top New York designers in 1946.

227

The polo coat, often of camel hair, is about as timeless a style as can be found. The sash holds the buttonless wraparound in place. It is casual, snug and chic. No wonder it's lasted.

I felt smashingly elegant in this yellow and gray checked coat, with hat to match (page 327). I even brought my gray Bedlington, Plugit, to complete the effect.

Here's that high, wide waistband again - I'd forgotten how popular that was - on an easy, flared white skirt, worn with a simple navy shirt, and topped by a bold plaid wool jacket in red and white.

Here's a coat of mine in an enormous wool plaid, in many graduated shades of blue. It went nicely with the suit on Page 219.

Double-breasted and sashed, this creamy coat would go with many an outfit.

"Plugit" again guards me, but doesn't quite steal the scene from this splendidly striped and full, coverall coat.

Let's say it was just mist, not smog that hid a clear view across the San Fernando Valley in the 1940s. I wore this lovely lynx-collared coat with not one pang of conscience. No one had yet heard the term "endangered."

As in the '30s, we liked lapels that were Lapels. I found this white wool double-breasted coat stunning.

MGM PHOTO By Clarence Bull

These next four pictures display how variations on the little "basic black dress" theme can be carried to an art form. On my head, a "baby doll" hat.

Charming as all these different touches are, it's important that the "basic black" be a beauty. Note the distinctive elegance of the dolman sleeves that taper as they descend to snugly fitting forearms, ending in scalloped trim that covers part of the hands. The same scallops at the neckline.

MGM PHOTO By Clarence Bull

236

MGM PHOTO By Clarence Bull

Shocking pink livens things, with the multilayered undulating pancake of a hat, matching suede muff-purse and gloves. And one great jewelled bauble at the waist.

An unusual circle purse, white gloves and snowy white flowers worn almost like earmuffs instead of a hat, make you memorable in this one.

MGM PHOTO By Clarence Bull

MGM Photo By Virgil Apger

Howard Shoup had fun glamourizing me at Metro in '42 for a highly affected, stagestruck role in "Seven Sweethearts." Shell pink chiffon, gold beaded bib and wide waistband, and tumbles of ruffles at hem and a slight train, weave the magic.

238

MH-53A

Interesting, how basically the same materials, chiffon and gold beading, can be worked to achieve quite opposite effects. Where Shoup made me ultrasophisticated at RKO for "Irene," Edward Stevenson achieved a look of rich ingenuousness, if not innocence. The short trains on both kept me discreetly kicking, under that fullness, to avoid tripping over myself.

Another concoction of mine, for occasions both festive and casual. Yellow jersey turban, yellow crepe blouse, multicolored striped skirt with rib-hugging waistband. And so I still have it!

Fresh and crisp for a mild summer evening, what could be better than this?
From Vogue magazine, May, 1948 (flawed copy reproduction).

MGM Photo By Clarence S. Bull

Good simple lines, a narrow gold belt, and a cascade of stiff white silk, wonderfully waved ruffles at the collar and down the bodice of a black crepe dinner ensemble, white silk cuffs emerging from the wide sleeves, all in superb good taste. I can't tell you who designed this one. Sorry! I just forgot.

It's just so gorgeous, I had to show it twice.

A fairy-tale gown! - more of Edward Stevenson's sorcery for "Irene" at RKO in 1940. Miles and miles of tulle, black over flesh, to give an iridescence to this superb ballgown. And again, the waistband is wide.

243

There's a story that goes with this glory of a gown.

Production of Metro's "Human Comedy" in 1943 found us in the very midst of World War II. Designer Irene wanted to provide me with a memorable formal to wear at a party that my very rich parents give, (and to which my new interest, militant working man James Craig comes without a tie). But alas, there were no fabulous fabrics left in the Wardrobe Department stock; all had been used up, and no more to be had for "the duration." American mills were no longer turning out luxury fabrics; instead, they were providing what the war required. All imported fabrics had long since ceased to arrive. German submarines, the dreaded U-Boats, were plying the depths of the Atlantic, on the prowl to sink any ship, be it merchant, passenger or warship, that dared to try to cross that ocean.

One lone piece of exquisite imported lace remained in stock, but it was not quite large enough for a whole gown. Irene put her creative gifts to work. She used every inch of lace she had to work with, and made a graceful insert of white mousseline de soie forming a long triangle from waist to floor, topped and edged with cascading ruffles. Thus, the gap was filled, and to make it look intentional, Irene placed full, rippling ruffles of mousseline at each wrist.

And voila! An entirely original style was born, and isn't it lovely?

A dinner dress to make any lady look lovelier is Irene's filmy white lace that goes over a pale nude crepe slip. Sheer white mousseline de soie cascades down the cutaway skirt to form a full underskirt; it ruffles softly at the wrists in quaint contrast to the sleek princess lines of the dress. Marsha will next be seen in "The Human Comedy."

Of Song and Dance

Here are some shots in Metro's "Unholy Partners," 1941. I played a nightclub singer and got to belt out a rendition of "After You've Gone."

I've no record of who designed my white chiffon gown, but the ride-out vocal arrangement was by Al Siegal, celebrated for having "discovered" and coached Broadway's brass-larynxed Ethel Merman to stardom (I never sounded remotely like her).

246

To help me sing "I've Got You Under My Skin" in a nightclub (for "Lost Angel" at MGM, 1943), Irene fashioned me a skintight white dream of a gown, draped and fitted in inspired ways, and trimmed with handworked scrolls of gold cord.

Like as not, with a few more curves, I might well have aimed my sights at musicals rather than straight acting. Heaven knows I'm as fond of singing as I am of breathing, and find both necessary. I did sing in four movies: "College Holiday," "Unholy Partners" "Music for Millions" and "Lost Angel." During my contract years, my best chums always were the songwriters and composers at those studios, rather than my fellow actors.

Here are some shots while shooting "Lost Angel," carefully listening to my prerecorded "play-back" of "I've Got You Under My Skin," memorizing the phrasing, then "lip-syncing" (synchronizing my lip movements and live singing to the playback) before a mirror, and then in performance in a nightclub scene. Irene designed the elegant gold-embroidered white crepe gown.

As to dancing, it has always come easily, though I never trained professionally for it. There was plenty of ballroom dancing to do in my pictures, but never a dance number. That had to be done impromptu, whiling away free time on the set. Here I am, teaching my beloved Margaret O'Brien a few steps during shooting of "Lost Angel." Couldn't you eat her up?

And here (opposite page) is someone a bit better equipped than I, to show dance technique. What was his name again? Not Kerrigan, not Kilroy - wait! I have it now: Kelly. That was it, Gene Kelly, teaching me a thing or two, between scenes of "Pilot #5", in which he didn't dance a step. (That striped turban I'm wearing is the one referred to on Page 195, worn earlier by superb dancer Eleanor Powell. Maybe <u>that's</u> why Gene thought of showing me a step.) 🍏

Aren't little girls dressing just this way today, 50 years later? - at least, for "cleanup" time.

250

We Also Serve...

In Uniforms

Not all of my roles wore finery. They also wore uniforms and worked in a lot of kitchens. One of my favorite roles was as a housemaid, in "The Affairs of Martha." In another, I was a cleaning woman at "Carnegie Hall." And whether cooking for a soldier date in "A Letter for Evie," or housekeeping for a warplant worker husband in "Joe Smith, American," or milking the family cow down on the farm in "I'll Wait for You" - I wore an apron.

The uniforms of services vary, of course. There's the smock to assist in a police crime laboratory in "Kid Glove Killer"; the drive-in restaurant's carhop uniform worn by Ava Gardner, also in "Kid Glove Killer"; the musicians' in a symphony orchestra, "Music For Millions"; as civvy companion to Air Force fliers in "Pilot #5"; the GI fatigues issued to women at Bataan in the Philippines in "Cry Havoc!" 🐝

As if posing for a tintype from helmet to olive drab fatigues to Li'l Abner boots, I'm smartly turned out by U.S. Army Issue for MGM's World War II "Cry Havoc!"

Leonard Carey was a very dear English gentleman who got caught in the rut of playing butlers and couldn't get out. But he was splendid at it, as you see. It's "The Affairs of Martha," MGM, 1942.

Barry Nelson, one of the best light comedians on stage or screen, is "helping" me prepare dinner. Another apron.

*"Martha" in still another uniform, reasoning with Barry,
one of <u>three</u> leading men I had in "Affairs of Martha"!*

War plant worker Robert Young and his missus discuss raising their son in MGM's "Joe Smith, American," 1941.

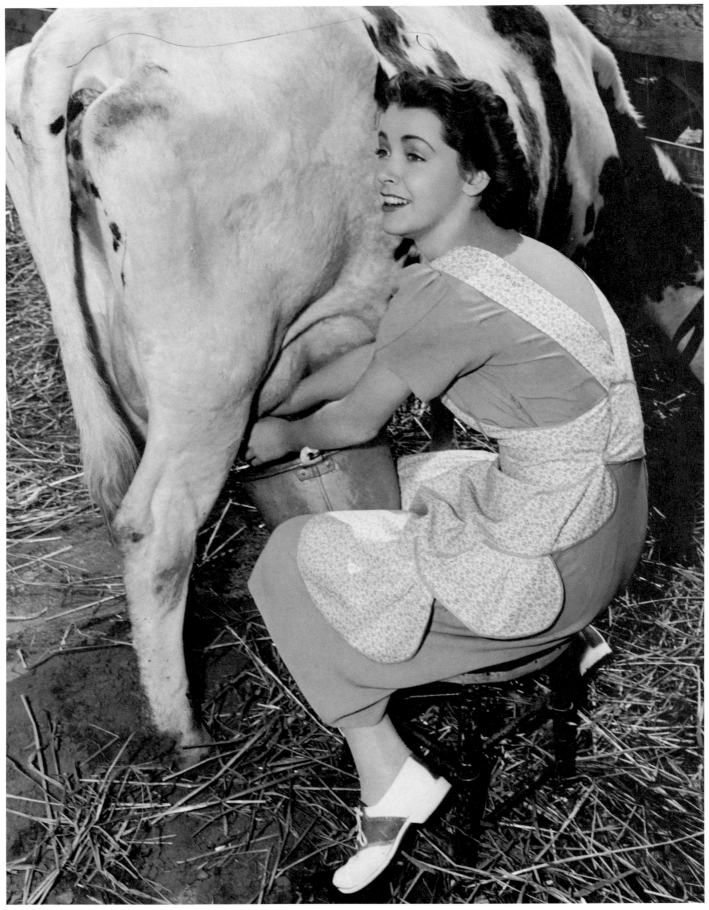

Yep, I really did get milk from cow to bucket in Metro's "I'll Wait for You," 1941. Not bad for a New York City girl. Remember saddle oxfords?

MGM Photo By Clarence S. Bull

Here's the title shot for "I'll Wait for You," parting from Robert Sterling, and in a different apron.

259

Assisting Van Heflin in a crime lab of the Police Department in "Kid Glove Killer," Metro '42, was a pleasure.

A good, roomy functional smock helped me look legitimately scientific in that crime lab.

The pretty, uniformed carhop serving Lee Bowman
and me in *"Kid Glove Killer"* is named Ava Gardner
in her first screen appearance.

262

"First time I've felt like kissing the cook since I joined the army," John Carroll tells me over the spaghetti in "A Letter for Evie," MGM, 1945.

In '44s "Music for Millions," an act of friendship is misinterpreted and witnessed by many of the symphony musicians, all in uniform for the coming concert. Margaret O'Brien, June Allyson, et al.

*This "Carnegie Hall" cleaning woman has
a confidant, maintenance/doorman
Frank McHugh, United Artists, 1946.*

Who wouldn't smile, between two such leading men as
Franchot Tone and Gene Kelly in "Pilot #5," Metro, '42?

MGM Photo By Clarence S. Bull

266

MGM Photo By Clarence S. Bull

Sing a song of airmen before "Off They Go, Into the Wild Blue Yonder." Franchot, Gene and I catch a carefree moment in "Pilot #5," Metro, '42.

MGM Photo By Clarence S. Bull

Fine actors, fine fellows, Franchot and Gene. The filming was over much too soon.

Mail Call at Bataan, the Philippines, it's Metro's "Cry Havoc!" in '43,
and left to right:
(front row): Ann Sothern, Margaret Sullavan, M.H., Fay Bainter,
Joan Blondell.
(back row): Diana Lewis, Feli Franquelli, Gloria Grafton, Frances
Gifford, Dorothy Morris, Heather Angel, Ella Raines.
All gorgeously costumed by Uncle Sam.

Here's the whole, all-female cast on the march.
From left: Fay Bainter, Diana Lewis, Feli Franquelli, M.H.,
Ann Sothern, Joan Blondell, Margaret Sullavan, Ella Raines,
Frances Gifford, Dorothy Morris, Heather Angel, Gloria Grafton.

Fully loaded transport.
Front: Fay Bainter, Margaret Sullavan, Driver M.H., Diana
Lewis, Ella Raines.
Rear: Joan Blondell, Frances Gifford, Ann Sothern, Gloria
Grafton, Heather Angel, Feli Franquelli, Dorothy Morris.

Angeles Times

MONDAY MORNING, DECEMBER 27, 1943   CITY NE

OFF TO TAKE CHEER TO NATION'S FIGHTERS

ON TOUR—Among 150 film players who left yesterday for visits to military camps and hospitals all over the United States are, front row, kneeling, Chill Wills, Mickey Rooney, Annie Rooney, Anne Gwynne, Marguerite Chapman, Henry O'Neill; standing, Fred Brady, Sir Cedric Hardwicke, Marsha Hunt, Raymond Walburn, Charles Bickford, Lucille Ball, Walter Pidgeon, Jinx Falkenburg, Reginald Owen, Signe Hasso, Francis Lederer.

Film Players Leave for Visits to Servicemen

More than 150 motion-picture players left here yesterday for all parts of the country to visit thousands of servicemen in camps and hospitals. Their des-

tinations include Seattle, Tampa, Fla., El Paso, Tex., Pittsburgh, Salt Lake City, New Orleans and other cities.

It was one of the largest one-day exoduses of celebrities from the movie capital since the Hollywood Victory Committee established its volunteer wartime talent pool two years ago.

In co-operation with the Victory committee and U.S.O.-Camp Shows, Inc., the War Department set up 80 tour routes which will permit each of the players to extend greetings in person to thousands of soldiers, sailors,

marines and coast guardsmen between now and New Year's Eve.

Among the stars who left yesterday or late Christmas Day were Ginger Rogers, Hedy Lamarr, Joan Crawford, Walter Pidgeon, Mickey Rooney, Dick Powell, Robert Young, Fred MacMurray, Wallace Beery and Carol Ann Beery, Franchot Tone and his wife, Jean Wallace, Irene Dunne, Lucille Ball, Brian Ahern, Charles Bickford, Jinx Falkenburg, Francis Lederer, Marsha Hunt, Henry O'Neill and Alan Marshall.

The Hollywood War Effort

When the Japanese attack on Pearl Harbor cried "Havoc!" December 7,1941, we finally let slip our dogs of war. Suddenly we found ourselves plunged into all of World War II, dispatching our young men, and even some young women, across both our oceans to play their life-and-death roles in a global theatre of war. At home, we scrambled to tool up for the fray and learned about loneliness and dread, rationing, coastline blackouts and civil defense.

This was a "popular" war, if that's ever possible, quite unlike any since. We had been attacked by Japan; and Hitler, already holding Europe, must be stopped before he took over the world. All Americans closed ranks, made sacrifices and worked together for a common goal: victory over the Axis of Germany-Italy-Japan.

Hollywood, too, went to war, waving off the studios' younger technicians, writers, directors and producers, and many of the public's favorite young actors to see service in all branches of our military. They racked up some very distinguished records.

War movies were made about the home front, war production, combat, subversion, spying, and refugees. I played in eight war-related films.* Oriental actors of whatever national ancestry saw steady employment as cruel "Japs," since our government had incarcerated all west coast Japanese and Japanese-American residents, visitors and citizens alike. Almost any European accent would do to play wicked German Nazis and Italian Fascists. For morale building, all the major studios turned out lavish musical revues, bursting with song, dance, patriotism and confidence of victory.

Studio publicists put their charges, the contract players, through

* (see page 292)

all the appropriate paces. If the number of civil defense pictures I posed for was typical, we all must have glutted the periodicals and press with "doing-our-bit" shots. My stored stacks of stills have yielded scores of poses showing home precautions to take, such as:

1. (a) Hanging black out curtains over every window to hide Los Angeles from enemy offshore ships or attacking planes.

   (b) Keeping portable radios nearby for emergency instructions, possibly to evacuate.

2. Keeping flashlights and candles handy in case of a power failure.

3. Filling bathtubs, buckets and thermos bottles in case a water main should break.

4. Having practical, warm clothing at hand for a possibly long hike to safety.

5. Updating First Aid supplies.

6. Stripping windows with tape to prevent shattering in a bombard ment.

7. Painting outdoor step edges white to find your way safely at night in black outs.

8. Lying prone, breathing through a towel comes gas or germ warfare.

The watchwords were, "Be Prepared!" and the studios showed the nation how. Here's just a sampling of them all, with me wearing a currently popular dirndl peasant dress.

(Continued on Page 280)

MGM's *"Panama Hattie,"* 1942, had a rousing, patriotic finale number called *"The Son of a Gun Who Picks on Uncle Sam."* With apologies to the unknown end men:

Front row, left to right: M.H., Red Skelton, Ann Sothern, and in front of her, Jackie Horner, Dan Dailey and Virginia O'Brien.

In the second you'll find Ben Blue and Rags Ragland.

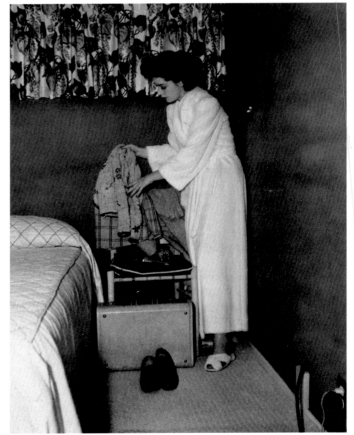

"Doing-our-bit" with civil defense pictures - the watchwords were, "Be Prepared!"

During World War II, I was married to a lieutenant and then to a captain in the U.S. Army. Both looked a lot like Jerry Hopper. Both were in the Signal Corps, based mostly at Astoria, Long Island, New York. Here, Lieutenant Hopper, on brief leave, pays his wife a visit on a set at Metro.

And here, about a year later, I'm paid another visit in my portable dressing room by Captain Hopper, who now wears a moustache, a distinguished touch to go with that added bar on his collar. Oh, I was proud of him! I'm wearing a brown skirt and cream top with stitching..

War Effort

I was no Betty Grable, Rita Hayworth or Ann Sheridan, the "pinup" queens, whose likenesses decorated walls of U.S. servicemen's tents and barracks all around the globe; but it seemed all my waking hours at home and between scenes on the set were spent hand-autographing and personally dedicating thousands of pictures to send to our military all over the warring world. It seemed little enough to do, and I looked for more.

Something new was formed for civilian volunteers called WADCA, the Women's Ambulance and Defense Corps of America, no less. I've no idea how it caught on nationwide, but around here, with our Pacific coastline so near, it was earnest stuff. Having a station wagon at the time, I enlisted it along with me, for service. If push came to shove, my wagon and I would help evacuate the San Fernando Valley! Just where to, I don't think we were ever told. But we were ready.

(Continued)

"Pupchen" and I, braced against a sandbag supply pile.

War Effort

We WADCAs did infantry drill, we handled cement and sandbags, we took Red Cross First Aid courses, and I advanced all the way to Staff Sergeant, with uniform stripes to prove it.

There were celebrity appearances and shows to do at Fort MacArthur in San Pedro, a port of embarkation, and veterans' hospital wards to visit, which took me all the way to Texas and Louisiana, spending three days at each hospital they were so huge. There were War Bonds to sell, up and down the west coast and on hinterland tours. There were speeches and visits at weaponry and aircraft plants and shipbuilding yards, commending all those tireless war-workers

(Continued on page 286)

No nonsense. My station wagon and I are ready to help evacuate the San Fernando Valley! Even my regulation shoes mean business

INVESTOR - Idaho Bill Pearson, former Indian scout, bought War Bonds and Stamps from Actress Marsha Hunt, left, a member of Women's Ambulance & Defense Corps. Miss Hunt and Chevronette Pat Hawkins also obtained Pearson's autograph.

Mae Clark congratulates Sergeant Hunt.

Marsha doles out coffee to her squad.

Capt. Gregory straightens Marsha's tie.

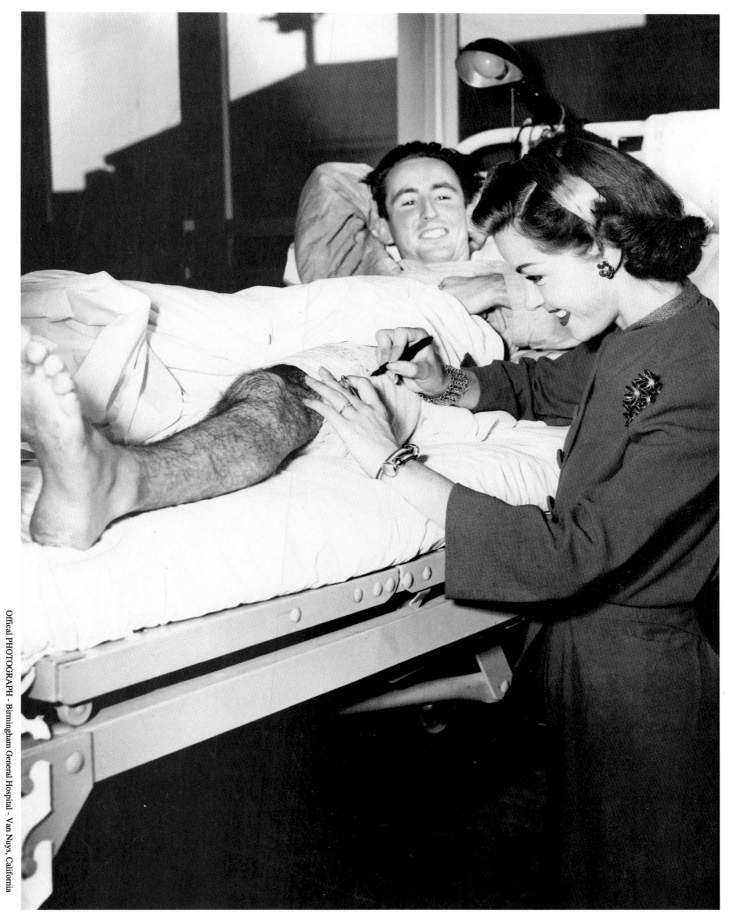

Easier to autograph this wounded soldier's leg cast, than his furry shin. I'm in a purple wool coatdress, headband and scarf in fuschia. He is in pain, but hiding it well.

War Effort

for their output, urging them on to still greater efforts, and even selling <u>them</u> U.S. Defense Bonds!

There was a lot of broadcasting over Armed Forces Radio, making shortwave transcriptions of interview chatter, poetry readings, all kinds of stuff to inspire, amuse and comfort our lads and lasses on distant atolls, fighting bugs and boredom.

I never quite figured out one assignment, but it was a fascinating challenge: OWI, the Office of War Information, was among, I hope, more important matters putting out radio transcriptions of hour-long dramas based on successful movies and with star players, on the order of C. B. DeMille's famous Lux Radio Theatre, "from Hol-lee-wood!" The difference was, OWIs were done entirely in French! They had long since exhausted the volunteer talents of Claudette

The huge lawn at legendary "Pickfair" hosted an afternoon mingling of military and movie folk. The foreground group, (left to right): Marilyn Maxwell, behind her, Jacqueline White, M.H., Frank Loesser in uniform, (later composer of "Guys & Dolls"), and Lynn Bari, licking her lips. Behind her, Andrea Leeds.

Colbert, Simone Simon, Gene Tierney and Ann Baxter, who either sounded or had excellent schooling in French, and they were searching desperately for more actresses who spoke the language acceptably.

One day in the Metro commissary I was asked to join the table of some visiting Free French dignitaries. To be cordial, and in all innocence, I uncorked a few phrases left in my brain from high school French class, and instantly, the OWI chap guiding the visitors coiled and struck. My accent, it seemed, was good. Flattery did the rest. I found myself laboring in two separate hour-long dramas, trying to get my speech up to speed with the otherwise all-French cast. I played opposite Georges Rigaud, a handsome and charming Frenchman I'd known at Paramount, whose career had never taken off as it should have. They told us those French recordings of ours played in 22 countries, and I still can't figure out why. ❧

Fighting men from foreign shores visit my set at MGM. Were they French? I no longer know. But the sailors' low-cut necklines were pretty exotic. And how did they keep their hats from sliding off their heads?

Phil Arden was a fine and cheery accompanist/companion as we toured military hospitals. His total recall of tunes and mine of words helped us fill just about every request for favorite songs.

This could be a stage at any Veterans Hospital in Southern California, Texas or Louisiana. We played 'em all. I wore simple, bright-colored clothes, choosing friendliness over glamour. It seemed what the fellows needed.

289

U.S. NAVY
OFFICIAL PHOTOGRAPH

Teamed as Mr. and Mrs. in "Joe Smith, American," Robert Young and I went up to the Naval Shipyards at Mare Island, selling U.S. Defense Bonds to shipworkers. I'm in the Mink, over a gray wool suit and green suede hat, orchid, purse and gloves.

Los Angeles, Monday, April 9, 1945

BOOSTER - Film actress Marsha Hunt speaks to Northrop Aircraft workers, aiding the Seventh War Loan drive.

It's a packed house outdoors at Menasco war plant - note rooftops - as workers, management, top brass and I celebrate their record production of 75,000 airplane struts. I salute the achievement, best way I know.

* War-related films I appeared in:

Cry Havoc!	for MGM
Pilot #5	for MGM
Joe Smith, American	for MGM
Music for Millions	for MGM
A Letter for Evie	for MGM
The Human Comedy	for MGM
None Shall Escape	for Columbia Pictures, on loan out
Bride by Mistake	for RKO, also on loan out

AFRS PHOTO

"One Girl and Two Boys," Three cut ups at an Armed Forces Radio Show. Ish Kabibble of Kay Kayser's orchestra, and comedian Pat Patrick have me hemmed in. My Egyptian filigree bracelet and the gold wraparound watch had almost daily wear in those days.

Checkered as can be, Georges Rigaud and I record our two hour-long dramas entirely in French (!) for the OWI, Office of War Information. It took all my courage.

The Mink

In a less informed time, animal rights and their sufferings were not a part of mainstream awareness. Sadly, a mink coat in those days in Hollywood was such a mandatory status symbol that despite our mild climate and my already elaborate fur wardrobe, it seemed important to have one. Not enough, that my cedar closet was fairly bursting with furs. No, there had to be a Mink.

I saved and saved toward the splurge. Noticing that there was a great sameness among mink coats - departing party guests, sorting through piles of them, had to find labels and embroidered monograms to avoid wearing someone else's mink home. I decided instead, on a cape. That would be identifiably different, and at once more casual and more dressy than an out-and-out coat. I. Rubin, the elegant furrier in the Beverly Wilshire Hotel, and I worked out a novel substitute for a collar. A circlet of skins ringing the neckline ended in two long loops, hanging free. Thrusting your right hand through the right loop, and your left hand through the left loop, you then grasped part of the opposite lop and pulled it through, thus forming a bow! It caused no end of comments and compliments. A rich, lustrous dark brown, with slightly padded shoulders, the cape hung straight down to an upper calf length. It fulfilled my wildest dreams of glory.

Photograph By Theodore R. Carstens - Los Angeles, Calif.

Snug in our de rigueur security blankets of mink, close friend and fellow actress Anne Shirley and I head for the bright lights.

But before committing myself for Rubin to go ahead and make it up, I wrote and drew a description of it to my then-husband, stationed with the military in New York, revealing also the cost. What did he think? Should I plunge? Back came a telegram in the cadence of the current Hit Parade top tune, "The Strip Polka": " 'Take if off, take it off!' cried the boys in the rear," Jay's wire advised: " 'Buy the mink, buy the mink!' cries your husband with a blink. 'Put it on, just for me, then come back and let me see.' " I did as instructed. And paying for it entirely out of my contract salary savings, I was certain it was among the very few mink wraps in Hollywood, paid for by the upright efforts of their wearers.

That was 50 years ago, and that blessed wrap has, as the song lyric goes, "been around the world in a plane," surviving the moisture of the tropics, the oven-dry heat of deserts, pelting rains and driving snowstorms, being crammed into luggage and luggage racks on planes and airport buses, surviving even being left behind on one such bus, found and actually returned! It's even been to the White House a time or two.

As fashion dropped and lifted approved hemlines over the decades, obliging furriers let out the skins for me, to lengthen it. Then later, distrusting the very short skirt style to last more than a season or two, I myself simply turned up the hem by hand; and was glad I had, when soon after, it was time to lengthen again, and all I had to do was rip out that deep fur hem. So we've had our ups and downs, my mink and I.

Don't let anyone tell you a cape can't keep you warm. In many a freezing city, I've simply closed my zippered hand slits and mushed on, impervious to howling winds in my little mink cocoon. Best clothing companion a girl ever had, and surely the best long-range investment. ❧

My most devoted fan, Bev Montalbano, greeting The Mink and me outside the stage door of a San Francisco theatre.

Next-door neighbor and "Affairs of Martha" leading man Richard Carlson and I take old friend Sergeant Jackson Chandler on a Metro studio tour. My new mink cape covers a beige shirtmaker dress worn with bronze accessories.

The Hollywood Canteen

The Hollywood Canteen was started by two remarkable people. One was the colorful reigning queen among filmdom's dramatic actresses, Bette Davis. The other was the founder/head of MCA, (the Music Corporation of America), then the largest talent agency in Hollywood, later to purchase and operate Universal Studio and its popular tours. He was tycoon/philanthropist Jules Stein. At war's end in 1945, profits from a film based on the Canteen came to $425,000, and Stein decided to bank it and form the Hollywood Canteen Foundation. Every year since then, the foundation has made grants to armed services related organizations, and each year, whatever the amount given, it was matched by the Jules and Doris Stein Foundation, thus doubling the size of the gift. This has been going on quietly for 47 years. In 1991 for example, $149,000 was divided among 37 Southern California veteran connected groups and activities, addressing the vets' many needs: financial, medical, and emotional. The Steins' matching gift made it $298,000. What with all the reports of greed and glitz, of shallowness and silliness that come out about Hollywood, I thought you'd enjoy learning about the opposite: an unsung, faithful act

have a snack, meet girls and dance to big-name bands such as Jimmy and Tommy Dorsey, Harry James, Benny Goodman, Kay Kayser, Hal Kemp, et al. It was a large old building, actually a converted barn, I think, at the corner of Sunset Boulevard and Cahuenga Avenue in the center of Hollywood. Everyone involved was a volunteer, whether in the kitchen preparing the refreshments (no alcohol), or dispensing them from behind a long, long counter chatting and dancing with the boys, or performing, M.C.ing, or parking cars.

I served as Captain of a team of hostesses, phoning and reminding 20 young women what their shift hours would be, and finding substitutes for any who couldn't be there. What Our Boys missed most at the surrounding training camps and ports of embarkation was Girls. And when they burst forth on passes, and seemed to head, to a man, for the Hollywood Canteen, it took a lot of rounding up of lots of hostess teams to bring supply together with demand. The rest of my family signed on, too: my sister Marge as hostess, my mother for food preparation, and my dignified father wowed me as busboy, resplendent in an apron he'd never have worn at home.

The Canteen held 1,000 men at a time, plus several hundred hostesses and helpers. Every evening on the hour, doors at both ends of the building were flung open, and the thousand lads inside were pushed out the rear door by the waiting thousand who swarmed in at the front when another hour's shift would begin. Each evening from 7:00 to midnight, as I recall it, anyone driving by could see a double line of eager uniformed boys on passes, stretching from the firmly-closed Canteen door, clear down the whole block, rounding the corner and well down the next side. They were, poor things, well accustomed to standing in line, and

SUNDAY AFTERNOON AT THE HOLLYWOOD CANTEEN

Reprinted from post card

of devotion to our country's servicemen and women, long after the welcome-home parades, that has gone on quietly for nearly half a century.

During the war years, the Hollywood Canteen was a wildly popular, free hospitality house for enlisted men to

they knew their turn was coming, to go inside that legendary place and maybe dance with a movie star. The Canteen was usually tended by at least a few famous folk among the other volunteers. Actors of all ages and categories liked to drop in, meet their public, chat or dance with the servicemen and sign autographs. Some performed

STILL in make-up the Erik Rolfs (she's Ruth Warrick) pass out chow, autographs, to camera-conscious G.I.'s.

QUIET moment at snack bar where Mrs. Bendix does her stint while Bill, below, is besieged for his autograph.

FAMILY NIGHT AT THE CANTEEN

Wives, Parents, and Kids of the Stars Lend a Hand at Entertaining Enormous Saturday Night Crowds of Service Men

MEN line up five deep for Marsha Hunt's autograph. That's her dad, at right, doing bus-boy duty; sister hidden behind waving postcard, and Mrs. Hunt, left. Big crowds made plenty of work for the whole family.

HUGE business in autographs keeps Bill Bendix busy as daughter Lorraine hands out soft drinks. (Bill's sideburns are for current role in *Two Years Before the Mast*.) The Bendixes, along with Joan Leslie and her sisters, are Saturday evening regulars at Canteen.

YOUNG Roddy McDowall, who can dish out soft drinks with the best of 'em, even has time to whisper in his mother's ear. Pretty sister Virginia at left. Roddy's at work on 20th Century's *Thunderhead, Son of Flicka*.

less glamourous duties. The supreme beauty, Hedy Lamarr, first met her husband, John Loder, as both worked at kitchen chores. Jack Benny, Red Skelton, Bob Hope and George Jessel, among others, would stop by, do a turn on stage and leave their audience rocking with laughter. Singers such as Marilyn Maxwell, Janis Paige and Georgia Carroll turned up to render the GIs' favorite songs. The starry list is too long to cite, but really the whole of

Hollywood rallied round the Canteen, as drop-ins or regulars. Case in point: Anne Shirley captained a team of Tuesday hostesses, which included the girl with the voice that saved Universal Studio from going under, Deanna Durbin.

The hardest night to get pretty and popular girls to come was of course Saturday, night of the big date with their own favorite fellows, hardly a time to do volunteer work. As for working actresses, Saturday was the one evening they could stay up and then sleep late the following morning, Sunday. We still had Monday-through-Saturday shooting schedules, and so most Saturday nights were booked well ahead for their own social events. Which is why I chose Saturdays for my Canteen stints, having an absent husband in uniform and with time on my hands. So I worked all five shifts of every Saturday night of the war at the Hollywood Canteen.

Sometimes I would be almost, if not the only recognizable young female face in the place for the eagerly searching eyes. And since every GI wanted to write home that he'd held a movie star in his arms - if only for a moment on a dance floor - it got pretty chaotic. Those were the days of "cut ins," when it was quite proper for a man, seeing a girl he wanted to dance with, to tap her partner on the shoulder, the partner then surrendering her. Usually the interloper waited at least halfway through a dance number before making his move. Not so at the Canteen. I was thrust every few seconds from manly bosom to bosom, clutched and released, clutched and released, with

a long trail lined up behind us, of waiting cut ins, snaking around the floor in pursuit, as each fresh partner tried to whirl and steer me away from the pack. Chaos and bedlam. We even had miniwars among the services if I wasn't yielded up promptly, with Navy challenging Air Corps challenging Army challenging Marines. These shenanigans made the dance floor a hazardous shambles for all the other dancers, shoved aside and trampled as this pursuit of a brush with fame took over and became a contest.

Finally, they grounded me. In the interest of safety, I, who loved to dance, was forbidden to. And bruised, breathless and disheveled as these skirmishes left me, I was truly relieved.

So for the duration, I was assigned a post behind the counter, presumably to dispense sandwiches, cookies and soft drinks. But our star-struck boys, denied a dance with a celebrity, insisted on some proof of a meeting: an autograph. I wanted to talk with them, but all I could do was ask their names, write them down with a greeting, and sign my name on books, paper napkins, envelopes, match cases, wallets, checks, handkerchiefs, belts and hat linings. No visitor to the Canteen would leave without the autograph of anyone there who was recognizable.

Flattering as all this attention seemed, I well knew it was nothing personal, that they weren't drawn as much to me, as to fame. I was then famous, but anyone else who was, would have done as well. Five shifts a night at a thousand autographs a shift, came to 5,000 signatures and greetings, and a few extras: "This one for my buddy; he's in the brig," and, "Just put, 'To Joe's Mom.' Wait'll she sees this!" Driving home, as I'd flex my aching fingers on the steering wheel, I'd thank the fates that my name wasn't Olivia de Haviland or Geraldine Fitzgerald - I had only 10 letters to scrawl.

The Canteen brought out an occasional sprinkling of WAACs and WAVEs, as well, proud reminders that women, too, were actively serving in the war effort. But most nights, our guests were nearly all male.

What impressed me was the boys' sweetness and respectfulness. Lots of horsing around among themselves, but carefully polite with me. How tender and young they seemed! For most, it was the first time they'd been beyond their home counties, and suddenly plucked from all that was safe and familiar, they had been put through a basic training wringer to emerge as

Reprinted from fan magazine

SNACK BAR does double duty when Marsha Hunt's on the passing-out side. Marsha hands out milk, doughnuts - and autographs - to the admiring crowd of service men and women. Her latest screen job, MGM's "Vally of Decision."

something called "fighting men." Thrilled, revved up and secretly terrified over the "great adventure" to come, many were on their last leave before shoving off, and cockily would promise to "get a Jap" for me, while I tried not to shudder. I've often wondered how many of those lads I danced with, and asked how to spell their names and wished "Good luck!" never returned. Or came home mangled by their great adventure.

Over the 50 years since then, I've come across quite a number of those Canteen visitors in all shapes and walks of life. We often exchange a searching look, as if in wonder, recalling our innocent cheeriness just before they faced the reality of war. ❧

Stargazing with The Beam at the Hollywood Canteen

Stars. . . Stars. . . Stars

. . . . , dozens of them made personal appearances at the Hollywood Canteen over the weekend, sharing the billing there with this post's 690 AAF Band, led by Warrant Officer Jerome Bredouw.

A photographer of The Beam had a busy time keeping up with all the stars at the Canteen but shown above are the outstanding enter-

Conte also was featured on the homesick. His solemn face changed movie "sergeant" who played roles

Photographs By Cpl. Jeffrey A. Trent
Beam Staff Photographer

doubled as Canteen entertain

Reprinted from Armed Forces newspaper The Beam, 12-30-44

Pictures of the '40s Social Scene

Barely into the '40s decade, the war changed our social habits as it did everyone's. With most of Hollywood's younger men and many of the fit older ones off into the various services, single and married actresses were left to pursue war effort events as well as their careers. A war wife whose husband was based on the east coast, I did just that, fitting in trips to see Jay whenever my almost nonstop shooting schedule allowed. I attended public events as part of a group, thus avoiding gossip columnists' leering surmises about any evening's male companion. Many of us, working full tilt on movie after movie, put our off-hours into some kind of war-related activity, much of which was social. Beach parties, picnics, dinners, dances and benefits for both officers and enlisted men kept us scrambling to touch all the requested bases and left little time for our old insular social life.

So instead, we did a lot of "sethopping," visiting friends at work.

FILMS' Marsha Hunt stops to chat with the famous designer, Lily Daché. The interested listener is Mary Pickford.

The ladies have no corner on the inalienable right to enjoy a choice bit of gossip. Van Johnson evidently gets as much kick out of a telling comment as Marsha Hunt, his "Ice Follies" date.

Marsha Hunt and Eddie Albert cut a rug. Marsha leaves for Eastern camp soon; hopes to see husband, Lt. Jerry Hopper, who flies back and forth between New Jersey and No. Carolina, where he directs training films.

My distinguished companion at the theatre is Earl Hunt, my father.

Marsha Hunt and Alexander Knox were almost late for the ""Dragon Seed" premiere, but they slowed down long enough to give us this cute candid.

Van Johnson's scars scarcely show. Companion - Marsha Hunt.

303

Reversing usual autograph routines, film actresses besiege British war hero Riddell. Clockwise from left of him: Patricia Morison, Virginia O'Brien, Joan Bennett, Eleanor Powell, M.H., Mrs. Louis B. Mayer, Loretta Young, Jean Rogers, Donna Reed, Ann Sothern and a mystery beauty behind Pat Morison.

One World War II lieutenant rose to become Commander in Chief of all the U.S. Armed Forces. Now that's a promotion!

Reprinted from Herald Express, Sept. 1, 1943

Photo and caption reprinted from fan magazine

Community singing was a highlight of the evening when Producer Joseph Pasternak threw a party for 10 soldiers and their "blind" dates - 10 lovely young MGM stars. These two lieutenants drew Judy Garland and Marsha Hunt as their partners for the festivities.

Photo and caption reprinted from fan magazine

Congratulations to Art for this super snap of this or any other season! An autograph hound has her arms around the man-of-the-hour, Mr. Van Johnson. Other celebs: Anne Shirley's at Van's left: there's Mrs. Keenan Wynn, Marsha Hunt and the Danny Kayes.

"Blossoms in the Dust" producer Lawrence Weingarten, my visiting chum Anne Shirley and I (in costume), hang on each word and await the punch line, when dear Jack Benny comes calling on our set.

Shirley Temple was not an MGM star, so it was an occasion when she paid our studio a visit and Judy Garland and Mickey Rooney gave her the Grand Tour. On the "Blossoms in the Dust" set, director Mervyn Le Roy, Fay Holden (remember her as Ma in "The Hardy Family" series?) and I welcomed the future diplomat.

Had Van Heflin's buddy, Charles Bickford, played more romantic leads, that splendid actor doubtless would have rated a "10." Here, visiting our set, he's coming on strong to me, with Van an appreciative onlooker.

ARMANDO himself explains the menu to pretty actress MARSHA HUNT, in town to play the leading role in "Carnegie Hall," which was filmed in New York, and her real-life husband, ROBERT PRESNELL JR., as they dine at Armando's.

We sampled lots of restaurants while in New York for the filming of "Carnegie Hall."

MARSHA HUNT and DOROTHY McGUIRE exchanged pleasantries before the curtain went up at the Ice Follies premiere.

Dear friend Anne Shirley came calling on the "Blossoms in the Dust" set and shared a tea break with me.

Comedian Eddie Bracken, father of two children, attended with actress Marsha Hunt and smiling Mrs. Bracken. You'll see Eddie soon again in "Miracle of Morgan's Creek."

310

Between his two tries for the U.S. presidency, New York
State Governor Thomas E. Dewey paid our 1946 filming
company at Carnegie Hall a visit. A spellbinding speaker, the
spell is cast over, (left to right): M.H., an unidentified man;
producer William Le Baron, (standing); director Edgar
Ullmer; his script-girl wife Shirley; Governor Dewey, and
another mystery man.

The Arctic Camp Tour

The demand for celebrity appearances at all kinds of war-related activities became incessant and insatiable, and so the USO (United Service Organization) set up the Hollywood Victory Committee to secure and assign enough willing and available talent to go around. It sent out word that entertainment was badly needed in the Arctic region. I had been hounding my MGM bosses to let me go out of the country to entertain our troops, and since an Arctic tour would require only six weeks away from work, my pleading finally won out.

We were a troupe of six, five females and one male, Reginald Gardiner. Only Kay Francis had done overseas duty already, as one of the famous "Four Jills in a Jeep" in North Africa, about whose adventures a film was made. We dubbed Kay "Sarge, our fearless leader." She acted as MC of our shows, introducing the rest of us and being breezily informal and anecdotal. With her distinctive raven hair and classic beauty, Kay was known for her fashion chic both on and off screen. She had worn so many gorgeous evening creations in films, no doubt her GI audiences expected more of the same. Instead, she usually went on stage in a simple dirndl skirt and blouse, but she couldn't resist trailing a long chiffon hankie. I suspect it answered the gnawing query: "But what shall I do with my <u>hands</u>?" just as pockets answered that question for men. The peasant-look helped her and the boys out front feel informal and anyhow, nothing could rob Kay of her own innate glamour.

(Continued)

Wise in the rigors of junkets, Kay traveled light, taking along only a couple of silk gabardine, superbly tailored skirt-and-slacks suits, with assorted blouses and sweaters. Her 5 feet 6 inch height had trouble, though, with her tiny size 4 feet, and when outdoors, we were kept busy pulling her upright after frequent slips and spills on the ice. Miraculously, these falls left her unhurt and cheerfully resigned to them.

Teddi Sherman, daughter of western film producer, Harry Sherman, was a singer of jolly, teasing songs. She had short red ringlets, great humor, and was round in just the right places above and below a wasp waist. When introduced on stage, Teddi, in a clinging jersey dress, would strut out before those sex-starved audiences, strike a stance, thrust out her stultifying chest and through a sultry stare would ask: "What's on your mind, boys?" while they fell apart, whistling, yelling and stamping their appreciation.

For Patty Thomas, who came as our dancer this was to be just one of dozens of camp tours. Soon after, she joined Bob Hope for years of global duty with his shows for our military, wherever stationed, in peaceful or combat zones. Looking like Li'l Abner's Daisy May, Patty's cloud of long blonde hair topped a pretty face and a perfect figure. Patty in dance togs was a feast for starved eyes, and she not only performed her solos expertly, she also took on volunteer GIs from the audience to dance with her. Having felt the weight of those clodhopper GI Arctic boots on her feet, Patty well earned the medals and honors she later won, and being called a heroine.

Nancy Barnes in turn looked like Shirley Temple grown up. Same dimpled smile, same fresh wholesomeness, and a fine and stalwart accompanist she was. If there was anything resembling a piano, in or out of tune where we put on our shows, she played it. And where there was none, she pulled out her accordion for our backup, as well as for solos.

Reggie Gardiner was by then an established film actor and comedian, but he had made his great splash in nightclubs and Broadway revues, doing antic vocal impressions of things like wallpaper, windshield wipers and locomotive engines, which he did for our boys with huge success. British, dapper and droll, Reggie's mock horror at our tour privations and primitive accommodations convulsed us, and we cherished and spoiled our lone male.

I went along as a singer. That simple statement masks an indescribable stage fright I'd long had, of singing in public, although I had sung in several pictures by then. It was the live audience that terrified me, and it was a measure of my patriotic fervor, that I had undertaken to face down my fear by simply having to do several shows every day for six weeks. I had coached my songs at Metro in preparation with the brilliantly talented arranger-coach Earl Brent - mostly ballads, with a novelty number or two thrown in. Sure enough, after the first couple of tentative tries, I found that I'd neither fainted nor thrown up. And emboldened by those uncritical, wildly grateful captive audiences, pretty soon I was stealing encores and actually impatient for the next show!

By great good luck, we proved a uniformly game group, cheery, compatible and even relishing the trying conditions of extreme cold, the bare bones dressing and sleeping quarters, long hours, fatigue, delays and boredom, making chitchat with constantly changing hordes of eager strangers, forever packing and unpacking, and living for six weeks in a cargo plane, lacking even passenger seats and consistent heating. It was our home away from home, where we repaired after each stop, to whisk us to our next one, and where we swapped stories, napped, read, set our hair, polished our nails, mended our costumes and worked up the freshness needed for the next port-of-call performance. I truly can't recall a single sour note among us in all that time.

Our plane was a C-47, which we named "Redwing" because its wings were indeed painted red, to help rescuers spot us from the air, should it crash or be forced down anywhere in those vast snowy reaches. Our pilot, Don King, was chosen to ferry us all over western, central and northern Canada and Alaska because he was considered the very best bush pilot in the Arctic. Certainly, he was, as far as we were concerned, and whatever the changes and threats of weather and flying visibility, we trusted Don to deliver us safely, and so he did, despite a few rather dicey occasions. He also was handsome and a fine companion, as were the several Special Services military men assigned to our junket.

We played to thousands of men at a time in huge, unheated airplane hangars, followed by immediate repeats to thousands more. We played in gilt-trimmed movie palaces in Winnipeg and Edmonton. We sometimes played to as few as 15 men in remote, isolated weather observation posts. And to all sizes of audiences in between, in every kind of bare or dressed up, overheated hall. We played to both U.S. and Canadian Air Forces, and once, in Alaska, there were Russian fliers in our audience - remember when they were our trusted and needed allies? - as well as a few German prisoners of war who'd been allowed to watch the show.

(Continued)

315

From teenagers to middle-aged family men, all were achingly homesick, wrenched by the war away from loved ones and all that was familiar, while undergoing training or just watchful waiting. No combat here, just dragging time, boredom and denial of even the sight of a woman for many months on end. Ours was the first live entertainment to reach nearly all of the bases we played, and so our coming brought the impact of an earthquake. For some men, the anticipation of just seeing and maybe even speaking to a woman again was so great they had been unable to eat for days. And since all enlisted seating at performances was first come, best-seated, hours before showtime, long lines formed outside the entrance where, standing and stomping in 40 below zero wind and cold, some worked up such a state of repressed excitement that they went into shock, and had to be led away to the Infirmary, missing the show they'd so longed to see. At each base where that happened, we would visit those girl-starved casualties after the show, and they were sheepishly grateful to see us.

We spent all we could of our time on the ground, visiting and eating with the men to give them needed companionship as well as the show. Their curiosity about Hollywood was insatiable. We danced with them in their "rec. halls," played Ping-Pong, and had musical jam sessions and sing-alongs. I almost wept when one solemn lad asked if he could stand near me. "I just want to smell perfume again."

Kay and Reggie, being a few years our senior, were the darlings of the officers, and accepted their invitations at social hours, while the rest of us mixed with "the men." There was no caste system among us; it just usually worked out that way, and to everyone's satisfaction.

At each base we visited, we were treated at dinner to the best they had. It was always steak, which they knew was

(Continued)

Top row, L - R: Dancer Patty, MC Kay.
Middle row, L - R: Singer M.H., Accordianist Nancy.
Bottom row, L - R: Comedian Reggie, Singer Teddi.

severely rationed in the States. The first week or so, we gobbled it down eagerly, but as the steak dinners wore on, we began to dream of almost anything else, just to break the sameness. You really can have too much of a good thing.

In Edmonton, we received our outdoor clothing: fleece-lined sheepskin parkas with hoods edged with fur, and bulky sheepskin parka-pants with suspenders atop fleece-lined heavy boots; also, of course, gauntleted fleece-lined leather gloves. We moved in them with about the same grace as fully-togged astronauts. Although lacking in chic, they were heaven-sent barriers against undreamed-of cold and fierce winds. We often kept them on, aloft in Redwing, to fight the chill.

Officers of the Royal Canadian Air Force briefed us on what to expect and what to beware of, along our frozen way. Whenever we were out of doors, even for a few moments, we must watch each other constantly for signs of frostbite on our faces. It could take hold in seconds. "A nose can go, just like that!" the officer warned, snapping his fingers. It would turn white. The moment it did, one of us must whip off our glove and clap a hand over the threatened feature, to warm it. If a hand started to freeze (numbness would be a warning) it should be thrust, if possible, against a bare belly - the warmest part of the body, he said - provided it could be reached under all those layers of clothing. "And don't wear two pairs of socks or get snug-fitting boots. That would cut off circulation there, which you need to keep your feet from freezing. You'll get used to a crackling in your nose.It's the moisture around the hairs in there, turning to icicles."

"If you walk any distance," he continued, "join hands, forming a human chain. If you don't, you could well lose one of your party forever down a crevasse. A crevasse? That's when, without warning, the ice you're on, parts, and makes a chasm sometimes so deep that you can't even see the bottom." I secretly wondered whether it might be better to lose one of us to that awful fate, than to form the human chain of linked hands, when any one of us, dropping suddenly into the crevasse, might well drag all the others down, too. And <u>then</u> who'd entertain the troops?

"In your visits to various camps" the officer went on, "you may come across some Eskimos and their sled dogs. Those huskies look like pets you've known, reminding you of chows and samoyeds and domesticated huskies back home. They're frisky, bouncy and cuddly-looking, and you'll be tempted to pat them. Don't. You could lose your hand. Just remember that each sled dog is expected to pull 50 pounds of weight, often at a dead run, for hours at a time. His Eskimo master feels he must be kept hungry so that he will pull his weight for those great distances, only if he is desperate for the food he'll get at the end of the run. That food will amount to only one slim fish, 6 to 8 inches long, per dog, per day; so, he's kept half-starved. And if he smells your nice, warm, blood-filled hand outstretched toward him, he's apt to decide that the fates have sent him an early, special treat dinner. So admire them all you like, but keep your hands in your gloves and to yourselves - if you want to stay handy.

"Now if you do meet and visit with Eskimos, you'll find them nice, cordial people. Don't come too close

(Continued)

318

When Kay Francis and her Hollywood troupe were in Northern Canada recently to play at United States army bases, Eskimos made a special monster igloo for the entertainers. Here, above, are two of the Eskimos who helped in the igloo construction, while Marsha Hunt, Reginald Gardiner and Kay Francis invite you to enter—on your knees. The troupe will be back in Winnipeg March 8 to play for service personnel for three nights running at the Orpheum theatre. Tuesday, the troupe is scheduled to play at Brandon and Camp Shilo. The schedule depends on the weather as the actors are traveling by plane.

Reprinted from newspaper

to them, either. Not that <u>they</u> might bite, but, you see, the most isolated ones sew themselves into their garments for the season, and they lead mighty active lives, so their garments get pretty ripe, particularly when you remember that they cure all their parka skins - and even wash their hair - with their own urine. So don't get next to an Eskimo unless you're prepared to faint, or you've lost your sense of smell."

There were other warnings, but those are the ones that stay in my memory. Reggie, of course, worked up that briefing into one of his more hilarious routines. We did indeed meet some Eskimos, who had built an igloo just for us to see, working through the night as we slept after a show. First came the dogsled ride, a fine slide over that endless, smooth snow world, and at a surprisingly good clip, drawn by those cuddly-looking, untouchable huskies. We discovered that they never barked, but talked a lot, in whining, strangled-sounding voices, rather eerie. Then it came time to inspect our custom-made igloo, looking like a huge double scoop of ice cream. The smaller dome, serving as windbreak, had the entrance, a low opening we had to crawl into. Once inside the main dome, we could just stand erect. We learned that this room was all-purpose. It was perfectly empty, but split-level ; the far one-third of the circular room was an upper ledge about 15 inches high. The two levels sufficed as furniture. Sitting on the upper ledge, they could drop their feet down to the lower level and thus it became a chair. Squatting on the floor level, they ate from the upper one; thus, it became their table. Moving day would be a minor matter! I remember my surprise at how light it was in there, surrounded by those thick blocks of opaque ice. Then I looked up and saw the "window." Neatly fitted into the dome was a single large sheet of clear ice, cut from the frozen bay nearby. That let in the light. Ingenious, indeed, this use of their stark surroundings.

I had crawled inside first, past the beaming, bowing Eskimo hosts at the "doorway." Then each member of our troupe entered, eyes crossed and knees wobbly, hand clutched to nose. They had run the odor gauntlet we had been warned about. I alone was immune, thanks to my heavy cold, which lasted throughout the tour. Like a fourth monkey, I could smell no evil. And so it fell to me, while the others kept a discreet distance, to compliment and thank those hardworking, kindly Eskimos, and to shake hands in parting, for all of us.

In one other case, I was grateful to that cold I had. In Edmonton, just before starting our tour, a Canadian officer noticed me hacking and wheezing, and took me aside. He handed me a fur throw rug made of marmots that he had trapped himself, clearly a proud possession. He wanted me to have the use of it during the tour to keep me warm in the plane, and to protect my cold from getting worse. It was a kind and trusting gesture. Self-conscious over this special privilege, and taking a ribbing about my "conquest," I offered to share it with the others, but soon had it all to myself for the duration. Oh, it was soft and warm, all right, as a covering for naps, but it gradually became unbearable. As the napper's body heat warmed the fur skins, they gave off an overpowering stench of urine, having been cured by Eskimos in the traditional way. With my congested nose, once again I was spared, and so I alone enjoyed sweet dreams beneath that reeking marmot rug.

(Continued)

Top Left: Aboard Redwing, Kay does her nails. Top Right: A quonset hut full-dress mess. Center Left: 40 degrees below, but there to greet us. Center Right: Sweet dreams beneath the reeking rug. Bottom Left: The grateful guys. Bottom Right: We were never lonely, and for a while, neither were they.

I'm afraid, though, that my cold proved costly in the long run. Apparently there's reason for the warning never to fly with a cold. It's said that's what impaired Howard Hughes's hearing. But I had to fly with my cold, not just once but daily for more than 40 days, and in a cargo plane, at that. I've had to ask mumblers to speak up ever since.

But costly or not, that trip to the Arctic remains a highlight of my life, for adventure, scenic beauty, danger, comradeship, the vanquishing of my singing nerves, and most of all, for feeling <u>useful</u>. I realized that a career in motion pictures was the lucky gratification of a rather selfish wish to perform as an actress. I hadn't also realized before, how much movies mean to their audiences, and how a player seen often on the screen becomes a kind of friend-in-common with everyone else. Thus, to meet a familiar actress in person, way up in the Arctic Circle was to find a link with all else that was familiar, a link, in short, with home. Back flooded memories of seeing her movies with one's best girl, buddy, or family. That link brought a kind of warmth to the chill surroundings, a kind of reassurance to isolated, lonely men who, more than anything else, longed for home. To be able to put my own temporary limelight to such effect made that limelight seem worthwhile indeed.

One last matter. I had hated war intensely, from the first I'd ever heard about it. As a sensitive child, I had often cried myself to sleep just picturing hordes of people forced to hurt and kill each other. War seemed to me the ultimate madness, the ultimate evil in the world. I've kept that belief. If anything, it was re-inforced on that tour, although we were far from combat. Besides the training and waiting men we entertained, there were the other soldiers and sailors we saw, when we visited veterans' hospitals in Canadian cities. There, in ward after ward, on floor after floor, lay the still breathing, still pulsating human junkyard of war, the relics of World War I. They had existed like that as long as I had been alive - for 25 years! Some were cheery, others vacantly staring, these twisted, dismembered, emaciated "survivors." Hard to believe, they had been eager and cocky young warriors who sang "Over There!" in lusty unison, but whose Over There had returned them mangled for life, robbed forever of all a man should experience and enjoy. They would wait out all the long years left for them in pain and privation, helplessly waiting for the merciful release of death. ❦

Hats –
and Hats Off

Hats, besides serving as our heads' protection from wind, sun, rain and snow, served long as a basic for the well-attired woman on the go and at daytime social events. Of evenings, small, seductive wisps of veils, flowers, ribbons or feathers, in just the

suggestion of a hat, often graced a dining-out or theatre-going costume. Besides, by day or night, nothing was more helpful in conveying an impression of the wearer, in establishing age, character, personality and even mood, to the beholder. Best of all, hats usually were flattering.

Of course, I can't speak for the rest of the nation, but around New York and Hollywood, I noticed more and more women going hatless during the '40s. Hats were surely still around, but less often on younger women, and then they were apt to be special ones, not just ordinary head coverings. It was as if the girls decided: If I'm going to wear a hat, it might as well be A Hat!

Thus, we wore cartwheel picture hats, veiled come-hither hats, Panama straw hats, berets, pillboxes, beanies, wimple-draped hats, turbans, slouch-brimmed felts and perky Tyrolean felts, tiny doll hats, and anything else becoming and striking that came along.

It was probably the last-gasp decade for hats as customary wear, and though I've enjoyed the liberation, I have missed them. 🐦

Pictures of '40s Hats

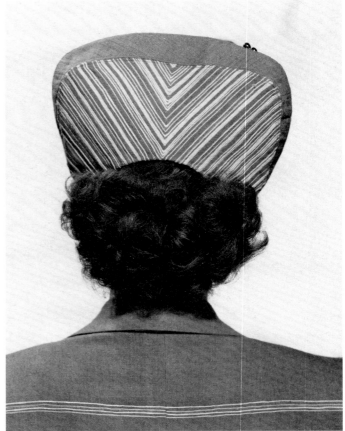

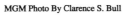

MGM Photo By Clarence S. Bull

MGM Photo By Clarence S. Bull

Photo By Christy & Shepherd Photographers - Hollywood, Calif.

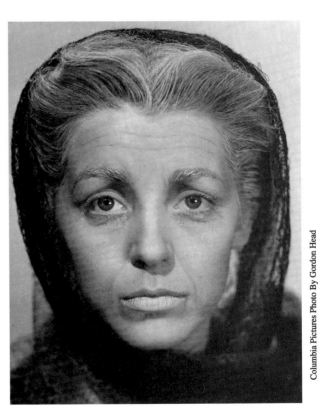

Here's a close-up of that John Fredericks hat shown on page 227. Lovely style for "an older woman" in 1946.

"None Shall Escape" in 1943 gave me another aging role. Set in wartime Poland, my head covering is a scarf, not a hat.

Columbia Pictures Photo By Gordon Head

Color-conscious Marsha wears her cyclamen suit when selecting a felt bonnet to match.

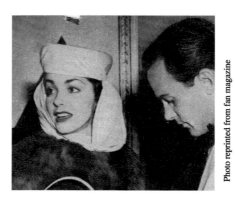

With Richard Carlson, signing autographs.

A purple scarf adds a rich note to this two-tone gray suit. The hat is of beaver felt.

Washington Herald

May 6, 1946

Inside Hollywood – Marsha Hunt, a Washington pretty who made good in cinemaland, adjusts her chapeau at restaurant LaRue as her husband, Robert Presnell Jr., obligingly holds the mirror.

Marsha Hunt, Hollywood veteran of the movie, "The Human Comedy," as she appeared yesterday upon arriving in Chicago from Hollywood.

Dropping in for a dish of curry, Marsha Hunt, actress, and Robert Galer are pictured at the Club Bali, East Indies night club in Hollywood.

Installs Mother - Mrs. Minabel Hunt, the new president of Motion Picture Mothers, is seen with her daughter, Marsha Hunt, left, motion-picture star, who installed her mother and other officers at the recent annual luncheon of this philanthropic group.

When two girls start talking fashions, what chance has a poor male? Marsha Hunt, left, and Anne Shirley, screen actresses, are shown in a huddle at the Hollywood Brown Derby, with the latter's husband John Payne, in between. The Paynes were hosts at the cafe following party at their home.

And Then the Bride Wore....

My second marriage was in 1946 to Robert Presnell, Jr., then a radio writer-director and screenwriter, later also a TV writer and novelist. This time the wedding was at a friend's house, performed by my childhood minister from New York before about 30 closest friends and family. And here's the happy pair who lasted.

Should you be curious as to how they weathered 40 years with each other, a following shot shows them on the night she first thought of putting this book together. 🍂

The bride wore a wide grin and a two-piece wool suit of dusty pink, the sleeves trimmed with double rings of matching fox fur. Her bridal hat was designed by her friend Sydney Guilaroff, chief hair stylist at MGM. The groom wore a wide grin, above a brown silk gabardine suit with a green suede tie that he nearly wrecked, trying to coax it into a Windsor knot. But the important knot; the marriage one, stayed tied.

The groom is 32, the bride 29 - good ages to start a life together. Ours lasted as a joyous, deeply companionable adventure for 40 years, until his death in 1986.

The Presnells attending the premiere of the Sherman Oaks Galleria in 1980, when Robert was 66, and I was 63. A law unto himself, my man refused to wear a tux, or even a tie, sometimes. Here he chooses instead a navy blazer and ascot scarf. Amazingly, he got away with it and never was challenged. A man of immense charm, wit, dash and charisma, he somehow seemed the best-dressed man in the room!

On The Air

Somehow, I never felt right about accepting payment for acting on radio programs. It was such fun, and compared to all the effort on the visual in movies, so easy! Happily for me, I did a lot of it in those pretelevision days, as did lots of "name" players from pictures. The network programs reached many millions of listeners, and, the movie bosses hoped, reminded those millions to go to see "this week's radio guest star" in his or her latest movie. Lux Radio Theatre, Screen Guild Playhouse, Silver Theatre, Danger, Suspense and several more had guest star formats. The prestige ones performed in Vine Street theatres before live audiences. There was always an air of excitement about it, like opening night of a play. Unlike filming - which could always go for another take when anything went wrong during the shooting of a scene - radio acting went right out over the airwaves, "live," tongue twister flubs and all.

It was a privilege to work in the company of the small group of radio regulars, those multivoiced masters of all accents and dialects, vocal chameleons who could and did play anything. An added treat was the chance to work with guest stars from other studios than my own, people I hadn't known but much admired from their films, Humphrey Bogart, for instance.

In 1948 I became a regular on the Edgar Bergen/ Charlie McCarthy Show, playing a shrewish wife opposite Don Ameche in a broadly comic weekly sketch called "The Bickersons." Gentlemanly Ray Noble led the show's orchestra, and was a hero of mine for the lovely songs he had written, such as Goodnight, Sweetheart, Love Locked Out and Love is the Sweetest Thing.

My 1936 debut in radio was somewhat inglorious. "Alice Adams," the Hepburn hit movie was to be broadcast on the Lux Radio Theatre with Claudette Colbert, Fred MacMurray and Walter Connelly as its stars, and I was to play a featured role. Just before rehearsals began, my agent called to say that the show's budget was overdrawn, what with three star salaries already committed, and he didn't want to establish a salary precedent for me at the low figure which was left for my role. Would I then forego <u>any</u> salary and accept instead a fine gift, so that the next time he could demand a proper salary for my services? I agreed, and was rewarded with a service-for-twelve set of Royal Doulton china in a pattern and color scheme I didn't care for, and with nary a bread-and-butter plate. A day or two into rehearsals, my agent called again to say that for me to receive closing credit as simply among the supporting cast, would set another bad precedent, making it more difficult for me to be starred later, and so would I mind working anonymously just this once, under an assumed name? Still young and thrilled at working with such stellar talents, I again agreed. And so, for an incomplete set of china, "Georgette Spelvin" made her radio debut that night. Marsha Hunt's was yet to come. 🍃

When Bergen-McCarthy program returned to the air in fall 1948, they featured the comical *Bickersons* skit, once heard on the Frank Morgan show. Don Ameche is star - but new Mrs. B. is Marsha Hunt.

"The Bickersons" - bickering.

TWO TALENTED HEADS TOGETHER. CBS Director Bill Spier discusses Suspense script with Marsha Hunt, at work after honeymoon.

Robert Walker and Marsha Hunt go over their script for the Cavalcade of America show.

SCRIPT GAZING Not wasting any time getting back in the old groove, Jimmy Stewart's been knocking off radio appearances like mad since he hit Civvy Street again. But by the looks of his collar it must have been a warm night when he guest-starred with Marsha Hunt on the Lux show. Or could it be Hollywood's hero is more at home up in the air than on the other? After resting up a bit as Hank Fonda's house guest, Jimmy goes into the RKO-Capra film, *It's a Wonderful Life*, for his return screen bow. Marsha's just polished off a job in MGM's *A Letter for Evie*.

Director Marc Daniels instructs Judy Holliday, Richard Hart, Marsha Hunt, Paul Stewart in "She Loves Me Not."

Pictures of '40s Hairstyles

Let's start off our '40s hairstyles with that basic "feather cut" devised by MGM's Sydney Guilaroff. The curls are about 4 inches long, the smooth crown a bit longer. You'll see, on the following pages, many variations on that theme, wrought by imagination and highly talented brush wielding.

342

MGM Photo By Clarence S. Bull

Yep, I confess. Seems to me my hair was a bit longer when we took this shot. It grows an inch a month.

MGM Photo By Virgil Apger

In *"A Letter For Evie,"* with GI Hume Cronyn,
Pamela Britton wears a coronet of her blonde braids,
softened with bangs. I have a short page boy.

Honest, it truly was still short for this style, and it took some "ratting," to fill out those rolls and make them look like long hair.

More short hair, say the experts, but short in a modified fashion. Like this coiffure worn by Marsha Hunt, star of Universal's Smash-Up. All it requires is expert cutting plus a soft permanent on the ends. And daily brushing and frequent shampoos to keep hair shining.

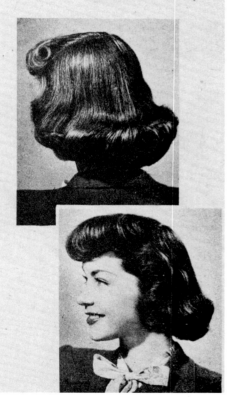

Reprinted from fan magazine

There's nothing like a new hairdo to give you a lift. It puts a new face on the world and on you. Here Marsha Hunt of Smash-Up wears a very new arrangement created for Woman's Home Companion by Hollywood hair stylist Carmen Dirigo.

Photo and caption is reprinted from Woman's Home Companion

MGM Photo

The one-name Willinger took this wholesome
and smiling portrait with its ingenue hairstyle
at Metro, before some more disheveled, sultry
shots.

MGM Photo By Willinger

And here is one of
Willinger's "glamour"
shots. All it took was
a brush.

MGM Photo By Willinger

352

©1949 Universal Pictures Co.

Now I'm in New York, 1948, and I've lightened my hair for the Broadway stage.

Hollywood Fights Back!

In 1947, with the war just two years behind us, some congressional and media opinion makers were telling Americans that Communist doctrine was at least as menacing to us as Naziism and Fascism had been, and was "boring from within." Our so recent wartime ally, the Soviet Union, rapidly became the object of our suspicion and outright hostility. The Cold War, not yet even so named, was about to begin.

The American Communist Party, still quite legal and putting up candidates for public office at elections, was numerically small, but contained a number of intellectuals and people in the arts, many of whom had joined it in the trying, frustrating years of the Depression. Certainly there were some in the film industry, and now their affiliation suddenly was made a furtive and shameful thing.

In the fall, the gathering storm clouds over Hollywood burst in a torrent of suspicion, confusion, accusation and fear. Some people back in Washington, D.C., were saying that movies often contained Communist propaganda aimed at subverting the American public's loyalty to our system of government and way of life. Those making these drastic charges were a handful of prominent film people, willingly testifying before a congressional body called the House Committee on Un-American Activities, (HUAC), to express their fears. Those sensational charges made in Washington caused a furor, holding the headline attention of press and radio across the land, while moviegoers wondered if their entertainment had turned into dangerous propaganda. Hollywood as a whole was appalled and outraged at such distortion, and film workers saw their livelihood threatened, if the public stopped going to movies.

Then, 19 well-known film people, writers, directors and an actor, were subpoenaed to testify in Washington before HUAC, where they were asked to admit, under oath, to any Communist Party membership, past or present, and that of anyone they knew. This seemed to defy our prized secret ballot and to make membership in a still-legal political party a matter of guilt, admission of which now surely would cost anyone his respectability and his job. Government censorship over the content of films loomed as a real possibility.

26 Film Figures Fly to Protest House Red Probe

Getting airline tickets at Los Angeles for flight for Washington here are (l. to r.) June Havoc, Marsha Hunt, Humphrey Bogart, Lauren Bacall, Evelyn Keyes and Paul Henreid.

HOLLYWOOD, Oct. 26 (U.P.) - Twenty-six movie stars, directors and press agents led by Humphrey Bogart left by plane for Washington today to protest a House committee's investigation of alleged Communism in Hollywood. Their chartered plane left the Los Angeles municipal airport at 7:45 A.M. (10:45 A.M. New York Time). Landings were scheduled for Kansas and the party was due to reach Washington tonight. The group represents the Hollywood Committee for the First Amendment. "We're just Americans who believe in constitutional democratic government," a group statement said. "We're protesting the nature of this hearing, because individuals have the right to be free from political inquisition. And we resent any attempt by law or intimidation to censor the movies as a medium of free expression."

Meanwhile, back in Hollywood a ground swell of indignation became a roar. Something must be done to counter the scare headline grabbing by HUAC and its chairman, to protest their high-handed procedures, and to defend our industry and its film product. A rally was held at the jam-packed Los Angeles Shrine Auditorium. Two hour-long, prime time network broadcasts went out a week apart over ABC radio, featuring short and pithy statements by a Who's Who galaxy of top Hollywood talent, under the program title: "Hollywood Fights Back!"; and to cap it all, a transport airliner was chartered to fly its planeload of volunteering film people right into the eye of the storm to our nation's capitol to hold press conferences expressing concern, and to attend the HUAC hearings at the House of Representatives. Howard Hughes, certainly a capitalist, and hardly a Communist sympathizer, offered the free loan of one of his airliners for the trip, but an FAA ruling forbade that, and so a plane was rented with contributions from all over the industry. Certainly no one aboard was in any need of publicity, much less of controversy. But it seemed the time to fight fire with fire, negative headlines with positive ones.

My screenwriter husband Robert and I joined in all these efforts. Neither of us knew much or cared about Communism, but American citizens' rights were being trampled, and our own motion picture industry was under unfair attack, and so we sprang to its defense. In the rapidly worsening political climate that followed, that gesture proved costly indeed. It literally cost careers, until and unless we later disavowed party membership, as many did, in order to work again.

Today it seems unbelievable that an industry would unite to punish its defenders, but That is exactly what happened. The studio heads were ordered by their banks to rid their industry not only of all Communists, but also of even suspected "fellow travelers." By having made these gestures, I was now so judged.

355

Gregory Peck, Dorothy McGuire, Danny Kaye, Fredric March, Hurd Hatfield (half hidden).

I stubbornly held out against "repenting," and refusing to say, under oath, that I now realized our whole effort had been masterminded by Communists. Of course it had not. But such an affidavit, I was told, would be the price of ever working again in films.

And so, along with uncounted others, I became "unemployable," as the Hollywood Blacklist gradually took its hold over the entire town. By 1951, it was in firm control over who worked and who didn't work in the studios, as well as in radio and that bumptious newcomer, television. I had worked in 54 films by then over a 16-year span. Since then, over the past 40 years, I have worked in only 7 films. Stubbornness comes high. But luckily and unaccountably, Robert was never asked to "repent," and was never blacklisted.

Calling ourselves The Committee for the First Amendment, those of us who flew to Washington were simply those who were not then tied up in production, among many more who wanted to go, but were busy shooting films. We were Robert Ardrey, Lauren Bacall, Humphrey Bogart, Geraldine Brooks, Richard Conte, Philip Dunne, Anne Frank, Melvin Frank, Ira Gershwin, Sheridan Gibney, Betty Hayden, Sterling Hayden, June Havoc, Paul Henreid, David Hopkins, John Huston, Marsha Hunt, Danny Kaye, Gene Kelly, Evelyn Keyes, Ernest Pascal, Robert Presnell, Jr., Henry Rogers, Joseph Sistrom, Shepperd Strudwick, Jane Wyatt.

The idea for the flight came from directors William Wyler, John Huston and Philip Dunne - neither Communists nor Communist dupes. Willie wasn't free to go along, but the other two acted as our leaders and chief spokesmen. As all the junket members gathered at Willie Wyler's house for a briefing, we were advised to dress for this mission, not as Hollywood people, but as Concerned Citizens. They recommended conservative suits for the men and simple, tailored outfits for the women. Here's how we looked: ❦

NOTE: For the complete list of Industry people who were involved in "Hollywood Fights Back!", see page 416.

Cover key: 1. Marsha Hunt; 2. Richard Conte; 3. June Havoc; 4. Philip Dunne; 5. John Huston; 6. Humphrey Bogart; 7. Paul Henreid; 8. Lauren Bacall; 9. Evelyn Keyes; 10. Danny Kaye; 11. Jane Wyatt; 12. Geraldine Brooks.
Photo by Martha Holmes/LIFE magazine © Time Warner Inc.

A JOURNAL OF THE FOUNDATION FOR THE U.S. CONSTITUTION

CONSTITUTION

Volume 4/No. 3   Fall/1992

HOLLYWOOD AND THE FIRST AMENDMENT

A delegation of the movie industry's Committee for the First Amendment poses at the Capitol in 1947.

Other delegation members unidentified in the magazine's Cover Key at left are: Robert Presnell, Jr., Shepperd Strudwick, Ira Gershwin, Jerry Adler, David Hopkins, Sterling Hayden.

Constitution Magazine cover and Life Magazine photo reprinted with permission.

Production Stills from '40s Films

Left to right: May Robson and Billie Burke, two treasures of American film, exchange gossip as Alan Marshall and I look on. Edward Stevenson designed all our finery for "Irene," starring England's Anna Neagle, RKO, 1940.

Just released from reform school, I bid good-bye to chum Laraine Day in MGM's 1940 "The Trial of Mary Dugan." I'm in street dress, she still in inmate housedress. Dolly Tree dressed us.

360

A few years later, Laraine (Mary Dugan) is an office
worker, introducing lawyer Robert Young to me, now a very
showy showgirl. It all shows how "Clothes make the girl."
Dolly Tree designed the transformation of costume, but of
course, the Metro Make-up and Hairdressing Departments
did their magic, too.

1175-42

As witness at Mary Dugan's (Laraine's) trial, I work on the jury with one pump kicked off. The silver fox bows over the toes were my own touch. Outfit: Dolly Tree.

In MGM's 1941 "Unholy Partners," Edward Arnold directs his famous scowl at Bill Orr and me. Little did he know that a few years later, William T. Orr would be running Warner Brothers Studio!

Now it's "Joe Smith American," also '41 MGM, and this time fine actor Bob Young and I are married and trying to pull our son's loose tooth. You're right, my hair didn't grow that fast since the last film. I'm wearing a "fall."

In "Lost Angel," Metro '43, I'm a nightclub singer taking no nonsense from my fellah, reporter James Craig, and it's in another of Irene's stunning suits, with checked hat to match.

Still "Lost Angel," who is Margaret O'Brien, and she's just been decked by a little boy billed as Bobby Blake, but you would recall him some years later on TV as "Baretta." Jim Craig and I are properly shocked. I'm in Irene's navy suit, with fagoting on skirt and jacket.

Now we move over to RKO, where Laraine Day and I were loaned out for "Bride by Mistake," an exchanged identity comedy, handsomely costumed by Edward Stevenson. Alan Marshall, center, admires Laraine's veiled big cartwheel hat, and mine is no slouch, either, of rippling multilayered net.
The whole outfit's a beauty.

365

Courtesy of the Academy of Motion Picture Arts and Sciences

More "Bride by Mistake": Though secretly married to Allyn Joslyn, (left), I'm instructed by my boss, Laraine, to flirt with Alan Marshall, (right). I try too hard and get very tipsy. Laraine's in discreet black lace; I'm in royal blue ensemble, with a pale blue blouse awash with spaghetti loops.

This would be "Kid Glove Killer," Metro '42, and I think I'm in love with Lee Bowman, who here takes me out to an elegant dinner. I'm in white crepe, with scrolls of flat, gleaming gold leather.

Moving on, same studio, same year; now it's "Panama Hattie" from the Broadway musical, and I'm teased/wooed by three inspired comics. From left: Ben Blue, Red Skelton, Rags Ragland. In this one, I'm a society snob, cold and chic.

Still "Panama Hattie." Here I lunch with handsome, endearing Carl Esmond. And how do you like my pagoda hat?

367

It had to come: confrontation with "Panama Hattie," who is Ann Sothern. (Hattie likes bows, and it shows.) Dan Dailey and Carl Esmond know well when to keep silent. And you get to see the pagoda hat's side view.

In "Pilot #5," still '42 (I was busy that year!) : fine actress Dorothy Morris played a tender, retarded young girl. I'm in a cream and cocoa dress. No, the shoulder straps didn't slip down. They were sewed to stay.

"No, Gene, let Franchot explain," might have been my line if Kelly and Tone and I had been playing ourselves. It's a tense moment in MGM's 1942 "Pilot #5."

Pure bedroom farce, wouldn't you say? Ah, but it's the '40s, and we're all fully clothed. It's Metro's 1942 "The Affairs of Martha," and Barry Nelson (L) didn't expect to find Richard Carlson (R) in my room. I'm in shades of brown, beige and cream wool, by Howard Shoup - and also in a bit of a snit.

369

In Metro's 1943 "The Human Comedy," Western Union telegrapher James Craig is a startled host to rich and flaky me. I'm stunningly turned out by Irene.

More "Human Comedy" with genial Jim Craig,
beautiful old Frank Morgan (alias the Wizard of
Oz), and Mickey Rooney at his best. I'm in another
of Irene's fine suits and a hat even I don't understand. Its veil's "got spots."

Time (1944) for Metro's "Music for Millions": Margaret O'Brien's found in the bass fiddle case by June Allyson in an expectant smock; Mary Parker, Ethel Griffies, a lost name behind M.H., Helen Gilbert and Kathryn Balfour. I'm in a former Katharine Hepburn robe.

Still "Music for Millions," and we're all musicians in the N.Y. Philharmonic Orchestra, but here, like so many expectant fathers, we crowd the Maternity Ward awaiting June's delivery. Too many to identify, but you see a good cross section of mid-'40s clothing.

Courtesy of the Academy of Motion Picture Arts and Sciences

Courtesy of the Academy of Motion Picture Arts and Sciences

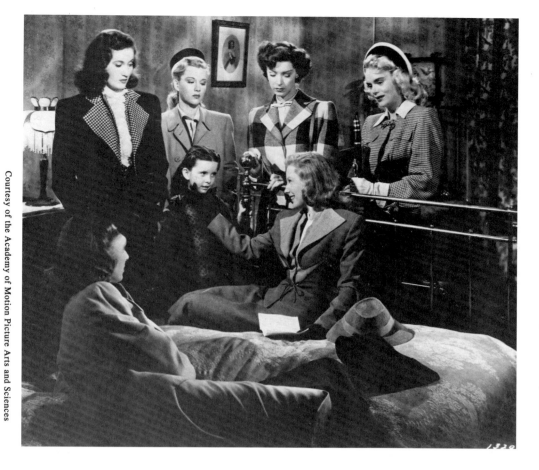

Check this out (four of us in checks): (left to right) Kathryn Balfour in checks, Mary Parker, Margaret O'Brien in a checked scarf, M.H. in big, bold checks, and Marie Wilson in small ones. Seated, June Allyson holding good news.

Lovers of teapots compare notes in "A Letter for Evie," '45. I'm in a pocket-accented suit, visiting Spring Byington.

373

1358-57

"A Letter for Evie," 1945, was Metro's W.W.II version of "Cyrano de Bergerac." Here, Evie (Roxanne) reads a love letter she thinks John Carroll wrote, but it's really written from the heart by Hume Cronyn (Cyrano). This was almost the only time in 24 motion pictures for MGM, when I wore slacks.

Here's the quandary: one girl and two boys, each with "A Letter for Evie." For this poster still, I'm in a pretty bead-trimmed dress, John Carroll and Hume Cronyn in their best Army dress uniforms.

Evie, ever so well-dressed on a wartime secretary's salary, is being courted by her boss, and she's trying to be kind but firm with her "No." He's Norman Lloyd, who went on to distinguished acting and directing over the years.

Still as "Evie," I'm about to learn that John
Carroll isn't the man I've come to love. (He didn't
write those lovely love letters.) My neckline and
cuffs are edged in loops.

Here, I'm loaned out to Universal for Walter Wanger's 1946 "Smash-Up." I'm singing idol Lee Bowman's Girl Friday, here with Lee and Carleton Young, going over tour plans. I'm in my own favorite vest of many colors.

© 1946, Universal Pictures Co.

Accompanist Eddie Albert (wrongly) suspects hanky-panky, but Lee is just praising my work, Carleton Young watching, and I work in a full-skirted but tailored coatdress.

© 1946, Universal Pictures Co.

The in-love couple, Lee Bowman and Susan Hayward, host
a party, and I'm secretly
envious. Her gown is overall
beaded shell pink crepe. I'm in
a golden metallic skirt beneath
a navy blouse and flame scarf.

© 1946, Universal Pictures Co.

Many parties and countless
drinks later, Susan as
"Angie," works up a suspi-
cious rage. She's in gold
sequins, and I in a white
dinner suit with embroidery.

© 1946, Universal Pictures Co.

379

Just to finish the sequence, here, the rage explodes. Angie gets her wish to see my perfect coif messed up.

It's still 1946, but now I'm a free lance and in New York City shooting "Carnegie Hall." Here, in my 50s, I'm proud of son William Prince, his musical talent and technique.

380

Son Bill Prince and I visit with the great composer/conductor, Walter Damrosch, 84 and blind, but he'd memorized all his lines, a true pro. The scene is my manager's office in "Carnegie Hall."

After a lifetime of service to that great concert hall, I'm about to resign, and Jascha Heifetz, the immortal violinist tells me, "But Nora, you can't leave. You are Carnegie Hall!" (I've been called the Hall ever since.)

381

Martha O'Driscoll, who loves my son, tries to end our estrangement, but I can't accept his turning from classics to jazz. My white wig is a bit lofty, but I liked the outfit.

Serious phone call for Edgar Buchanan, Allyn Joslyn and me in Edward Stevenson's windowpane checked white wool jacket over navy skirt: RKO's "Bride by Mistake."

©1948 - An Eagle-Lion Production Photograph

Things are tense between Dennis O'Keefe and me in what was finally titled "Raw Deal," 1947. My suit has a striped jersey pullover, the stripes repeated on my jacket cuffs and lapels.

©1948 - An Eagle-Lion Production Photograph

Escaped prisoner Dennis O'Keefe wants my home as a hideout, and I, in my very prettiest robe, am trying to refuse him.

383

Serious business, this "Raw Deal" for Eagle-Lion. Trim and chic Claire Trevor and I both would like to wind up with Dennis O'Keefe, but first, some crises.

6/8-5

This may well be my very first film murder, and I don't look pleased about it. I wore a huge-shouldered kind of trench coat for the occasion in the movies' best tradition. We're still in "Raw Deal"; the tentative title was "Corkscrew Alley." In 1991 a very different film came out, also called "Raw Deal," starring Arnold Schwartzenegger.

It's 1949 and I'm back at Universal to make "Take One False Step" star-
ring William Powell. We're two strays from MGM. Orry-Kelly designed a
stunning off-white costume with striped scarf and sleeves.

*Slim and stunning Shelley Winters goes to work on Bill Powell.
She's in a draped gold brocade. I'm in velvet and satin, all
thanks to Orry-Kelly*

"*Joy to the World*" and Me - On Broadway

1948 is probably remembered by most New Yorkers as The Year of the Big Snow - it lay deep over the city when we arrived, blanketing it in beauty and silence and traffic standstill. But I'll always remember it as The Year of the Big Plunge. By then, a veteran of 13 years of filmmaking, I had never acted professionally on any stage, and my initiation into the mysteries and challenges of live theatre was to be a starring role in a Broadway play, no less! Three enticements helped me find the necessary courage to take that plunge: "Joy to the World" was a comedy-with-message about the motion picture business. I'm happiest playing comedy, and I sure knew the subject. My co-star would be Alfred Drake (his performance as Curly in "Oklahoma" a few years before had left me still dazzled), and the director would be Jules Dassin - for whom I had loved working in two comedy films at MGM, "The Affairs of Martha" and "A Letter for Evie." I would be lucky and safe under his direction, in anything. And Alan Scott had written a good and funny play.

Beverly Woodner's Delicious Designs for
"Joy to the World"

Daringly combining royal and navy blue checked wool vest and skirt with aqua silk full-sleeved blouse, tiny white collar and red tie, the unlikely colors clicked together, introducing the character as a crisply feminine individualist.
The fitted vest had flatteringly extended shoulders, and featured the watch-fob chain dangling my Phi Beta Kappa key, credential of "a Brain."

So Robert and I forsook our newly remodeled, just furnished home in Sherman Oaks and moved to my old hometown for the duration, whatever that would be. With the help of everyone involved in the venture, it brought me beginner's luck, a totally enchanted experience, and proved the first of six starring Broadway engagements over the years, besides dozens of plays all over the land. I fell in love with live audiences, so long denied on movie sound stages, and I'm probably smitten for life. Surviving friendships were formed with the Alfred Drakes, the Bert Freeds, the John Housemans and the Jules Dassins (both former and present wives).

Among the many fascinating differences I discovered between screen and stage was costuming. Cameras come close to actors, and movie audiences, even in back rows, see whatever the cameras see, to the smallest details of costumes, enlarged on the big screen. But play audiences are as close to the actors, or as far from them, as the location of their seats. Audiences seated in back rows and balconies get only an overall impression of what is worn. Detail is lost, but contour and color are what count.

I had been in exactly 50 movies by 1948, all but 1-1/2 in black and white film ("Blossoms in the Dust" was in color, as was one sequence of "Irene"). Now, for the stage, color of costumes took on a new importance to the mood of a scene as well as becomingness to the wearer. And for the first time, I was asked to alter my natural hair color since its ash brown shade looked drab from out front. I obediently lightened it.

As the head of a major studio's Research Department, I played a brainy and independent idealist, dressed for the part by designer Beverly Woodner in four varied and becoming costumes.

This scene with Mary Welch in studio boss Alfred Drake's outer office.

Beverly gave them originality, a quiet dash, grace in movement, and a delicious color range. Here's a look at them, caught from out front during actual performance. Photography was and still is strictly forbidden to audiences, but Fred Fehl was authorized by producers John Houseman and William Katzell to take pictures. Abraham Mandelstamm, an elderly theatre devotee, always had special dispensation from the management and always sent prints to the casts. We loved him!

Even my flat-heeled pumps held a surprise: double ankle straps!

Next came a simple white piqué fitted summer dress, full-skirted.

Tangerine silk, softened by a floating panel down one side, and see how the built-up collar cut my long neck down to size.
Left to right: Clay Clement and Myron McCormick.

Studio boss Alfred Drake and I discuss a problem.

And finally, a wool suit of softest lavender, a pearl gray chiffon scarf draped over one shoulder.

Since director Jules Dassin had me kneeling before Alfred, and sitting on his lap, (see next page), Designer Beverly Woodner thoughtfully slit the straight skirt and broke the hem of the jacket line into scallops, to ease these positions. The demands on costumes of action on stage have spawned many an innovative touch of design.

Scallops and skirt slit help the scene.

Curtain call shows the large cast's principal players (Left to right): Bert Freed, Leslie Litomy, Clay Clement, Myron McCormick, M.H., Alfred Drake, Morris Carnovsky, Mary Welch. (Kurt Kasznar ducked out early that evening.)

More Broadway and Also TV

Starting with "Joy," I starred in four plays on Broadway between 1948 and 1950. The second was George Bernard Shaw's "The Devil's Disciple," with Maurice Evans, Victor Jory and Dennis King, and set in American Revolutionary times; so there are no '40s styles to show you from that, nor from the next one, Lynn Riggs'

"Borned in Texas" opposite Anthony Quinn, which had a turn-of-the-century Oklahoma setting. That one had a limited run, as part of a Summer Festival of plays. The fourth was James Gow and Arnaud d'Usseau's "Legend of Sarah" with Tom Helmore and Ethel Griffies, a contemporary comedy but certainly no fashion show.

As you can tell, Tom and I aren't seeing eye to eye, and I'm breaking up house - keeping together in Greenwich Village, and heading home to New England. It took an extra half hour pre-performance every evening for make-up to cover all my leg bruises from these nightly skirmishes.

I gave as good as I got, of course, but at least poor Tom's bruises didn't show.

LIFE

MARSHA HUNT
IN
"THE DEVIL'S DISCIPLE"

MARCH 6, 1950   20 CENTS
YEARLY SUBSCRIPTION $6.00

LIFE

REG. U.S. PAT. OFF.

Vol. 28, No. 10   March 6 1950

CONTENTS

LIFE'S COVER

Azure-eyed Marsha Hunt, who acts a pretty Puritan in Shaw's play, *The Devil's Disciple* (p. 53), scowls at ingenue roles. Says she, "Any resemblance between an ingenue and any person living or dead is purely coincidental." Out of her 54 movie parts, Marsha has played several wrinkled dowagers, is always scouting for meaty roles. She has done more television dramas than any other movie star, and as Viola in *Twelfth Night* was the first to do Shakespeare on TV. Educated in New York, Marsha has acted only twice on Broadway, but she has become a critic's darling and her many admirers among the reviewers form a kind of unofficial Hunt club.

The following list, page by page, shows the source from which each picture in this issue was gathered. Where a single page is indebted to several sources, credit is recorded picture by picture (*left to right, top to bottom*) and line by line (*lines separated by dashes*) unless otherwise specified.

COVER—PHILIPPE HALSMAN
6—CARTIER-BRESSON FROM MAGNUM
10—T. CARNATION STUDIOS
14, 15, 16—VICTOR B. ORTEGA
21—W. EUGENE SMITH
22, 23—LT. LARRY BURROWS—MARK KAUFFMAN—W.

70—CHARLES STEINHEIMER
73—FERNAND BOURGES COURTESY CITY ART MUSEUM OF ST. LOUIS AND BOATMEN'S BANK. ST. LOUIS—FERNAND BOURGES COURTESY CITY ART MUSEUM OF ST. LOUIS AND MR. ERIC NEWMAN
74, 75—FERNAND BOURGES COURTESY CITY ART MUSEUM

The stage habit was now well upon me, and by year's end of 1950, besides the four plays on Broadway, I had racked up eight other stage engagements in summer and winter stock.

Between all these, as Life magazine's cover notes point out, lots and lots of plays on live television, that new medium just getting started, and then centered in New York.

399

Early-riser Marsha dons a smart suit, gets ready for morning stroll.

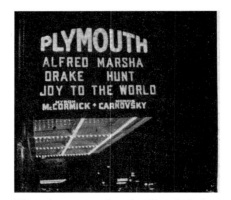

Yes, there it is - bright Mazda lights in the night.

Life for a Broadway star is different from life as a movie star in Hollywood. You sleep later, and you walk the dog that's in the show, too, for exercise. Life's easier back home in L.A.

A pair of Wedgewood vases - just the thing for her living room back in Hollywood.

Bob delivers his wife safely to the theater. His kiss is her good-luck talisman for the show

After the show at popular Sardi's, they eat supper. Bob feeds her - cameraman's whim!

Marsha pays strict attention to beauty details, she's always well-groomed.

In New York there is no sport dearer to a woman's heart than shopping. Marsha does!

Hubby, Bob Presnell, helps her select a hat at Leora Creations, Inc. He has fine taste.

Movie Star's Dream—Broadway Lights

You are invited to spend a day with that glamorous star of screen and stage, Marsha Hunt, and husband

★ Some call it a refresher course—other actors and actresses, particularly those who have experienced the thrill of a live audience—actually pine for Bdway. And one's name in lights . . .

It's more than a symbol of success. It is a dream come true; it is a life-long ambition realized at last.

Marsha Hunt, who stars in Republic's charming "The Inside Story" and is under contract to Eagle-Lion for a forthcoming picture "Raw Deal," has a hit show. She won't be lonely for Hollywood—it's about Hollywood.

At a night spot later, they have some fun. She adores "dating" her hubby.

And so home and to bed. It's 2:15 A.M. → and Marsha is ready to call it a day.

All pictures and captions on these two pages are reprinted from fan magazine

End of an Era

When would you say that a decade ends, after a year ending with a 9 or with a 0? In winding up the 1940s, clearly '49 is the last year with a 4 in it, but, on the other hand, '49 is only the 9th year, and so to round out a decade, the 10th year would have to be '50. Let hotheads debate the matter, but since there appears to be a choice, I've decided to opt for 1950 as the last year of the '40s, so that I can include it in this book.

How else could I boast about starring that year in three separate Broadway plays? Or my first trip to Europe? Or dining in Paris with Eleanor Roosevelt and son Elliott? Or buying two outfits in Paris, one a flowered silk that looked like a watercolor, and which I still wear, forty years later; the other, a Grés original, a gray and white tweed suit with cuffed pockets on the sleeves, yet which I hardly ever wore, a touch too original, perhaps. Or making the cover of Life magazine (page 398). How else to show it to you, (even if I was wearing a Colonial period, not modern, costume)? And realizing an early dream by renting a penthouse in Manhattan with terraces facing all directions but north, so that each privileged day and night, we could greet the Hudson River, with New Jersey beyond to the west; the famed skyline of towers to the south, and the green glory of Central Park to the east.

For me, a gala, crammed full, hardworking, intensely eventful year, just before the Dark Ages set in. For in mid-1950, an unofficial pamphlet called Red Channels came out with some fanfare. Careful to make no actual charges, it listed people in television and radio whom its authors suspected of possible Communist party membership, ties or leanings and, therefore, questioned their loyalty as American citizens. Networks and sponsors alike, fearful of controversy and loss of sales, took the pamphlet seriously. It listed me among its many suspects and pretty effectively terminated careers.

But the account of what followed doesn't belong in this time frame or context. The story of women's styles in the '30s and '40s that I set out to show and tell in this book is really told by now. But to glimpse the future from then on . . . . .

Our World Since Then

1950 . . . .

The way we dress today has been affected by all the things that have happened, the changes in our world since mid - 20th century, and so, to take them into account, some random recollections.

Just following the '40s . . . . and beyond: the intensified "Cold War" with the Soviet Union, stoking and bloating our defense industry for four decades. . . . the grinding 3-year hot war, called a police action, in Korea, that cost us 103,284 wounded and 54,246 killed, and who knows how many other fellow-humans? . . . . the widening search for "subversives and pinkos," that resulted in bandwagon blacklists that forbade employment. Blacklists spread through radio, television, motion pictures, the press, education, politics, the armed forces and even religion. That anti-Communist fever swept up uncounted liberals and non-conformists among its victims for well over a decade, now summed up as The McCarthy Period - so-called in (dis)honor of Senator Joseph McCarthy, the most showmanlike and irresponsible accuser of them all, who took on the U.S. Armed Forces and our State Department. . . . and yet, in contrast to that period of <u>political intolerance</u>, we saw an unprecedented growth of <u>religious tolerance</u>, inter-faith cooperation nationwide, though alas, more lately, a resurgence of hate signs; swastikas, burning crosses, vandalism, bashing of gays and Asians, threats and violence against racial and immigrant groups. . . . the entrance of the hydrogen bomb, fearsomely multiplying the force of what befell Hiroshima and Nagasaki. . . . border-defying, deadly fallout from nuclear bomb tests. . . . the spread of nuclear weapons possession from just us to five countries more, for certain, and half a dozen probables or any-minute-now others. . . . and to lighten the picture, Elvis. . . . the intransigent Middle East crisis and its sudden, brief wars. . . . the end of colonialism, with nearly 100 nations newly independent since 1950, flocking to join the United Nations, and diminishing our dominance there. . . . helicopters. . . . Sputnik and the race to explore space. . . . 3-D movies. . . . the Civil Rights movement and all the better-late-than-never reforms it brought. . . . the Cuban Missile Crisis. . . . "Camelot" . . . . Dallas, November 22, 1963. . . . the stubborn and growing suspicion that a conspiracy, and not a lone gunman caused JFK's death. . . . and so soon after, on his way to presidential nomination, Robert Kennedy's murder. . . . hippies and flower children. . . . jet airline passenger travel and how it shrank the world. . . . Project Headstart, for the disadvantaged 4-year-olds. . . . Jacques Cousteau, guiding us to learn the wonders in the world's deep waters. . . . Rachel Carson's "The Silent Spring," warning us of how we despoil our environment. . . . the vanquishing of polio with the Sabin and Salk vaccines. . . . the total eradication of smallpox from the face of the earth by the UN's World Health Organization, and its near-eradication of malaria, the world's most prevalent disease. . . . the hula-hoop. . . . our belated awareness of the world's frightening birthrate cramming our planet with more than double our numbers, just since 1950, from 2,510,000,000 then, to 5,587,800,200 as this is written, 6:00 p.m., April 30, 1993, but we must add 16,460 people for every hour since then, for that is our rate of growth. . . . the Beatles. . . . freeways and expressways that at first enabled motorists to freewheel our merry way, by-passing crosstraffic, but which soon clogged us to a dismal commuter crawl . . . . the traditional American Family becoming an endangered species, and our myriad social ills, as a result. . . . the U.S. landing on the moon. . . . color television. . . . Vietnam: the needless, unwon war that cost us over 13 nightmare years, 305,794 wounded and 58,095 killed, and who knows how many fellow-humans? . . . . the Vietnam War protest movement that divided the country, hastened our pullout, and prevented a president's try for reelection. . . . Disneyland. . . . pacemakers and successful human organ transplants. . . . adult education, allowing American grown-ups to return to school for self-enrichment, training and even for postponed literacy. . . . the decline of railroad travel, as King Automobile slurps up the world's oil supply insatiably, befouls the air and demands evermore thousands of miles of highway; these endless ribbons of roads attracting long commutes to work, and vast new suburban sprawls that gobble up 1,000,000 acres of prime farmlands each year. . . . a century-old staple for rural Americans, the Sears-Roebuck catalog folds . . . . the retreat from city residence by middle and upper income folk to outlying suburbs, leaving inner cities to minorities, immigrants, the elderly and the poor. . . . hair spray. . . . Martin Luther King, showing all the mistreated, the neglected and their friends that We Shall Overcome, if only we will, by peaceful means. . . . soul food and soul music. . . . mobile homes and recreational vehicles, lowering housing and vacation costs. . . . retirement communities, mushrooming in our nation's Sunbelts. . . . yogurt. . . . the Peace Corps, our proudest export, as the best among us give the best of themselves, teaching self-help in deprived parts of the world. . . . plastics, synthetics, drip-dry and wash-and-wear - the ironing board now all but obsolete. . . Laundromats. . . . domestic servants near-vanished from American homes. . . . surfboards, swim fins and snorkles. . . . the Generation Gap. . . . "Rock around the Clock" and the rock-y mountain of "music" it launched, its beat and electronic decibels assaulting our ears and nervous systems for decades, and no end in sight. . . . that takeover virtually banning melody and the charm of intelligent lyrics from the national sound. . . . the rock culture - albums, concerts and videos - wooing youth to worship mindless repetition, strident vulgarity, rebellion and the grotesque. . . . overnight millionaires from rock success - and yet, confounding their critics, mega-rock concerts to benefit AIDS, the homeless, world hunger, human rights, foreclosed farmers, and environment protection. . . . "grass" and "coke" taking on new meanings - they take over inner cities and suburbs alike - not to ignore LSD, and PCP, all those uppers and downers, crack, straight cocaine and the unheroic heroin, dazing and wasting Americans into the millions, and yielding pusher and smuggler fortunes into the $ billions. . . . and the legal addiction, alcohol, right up there as a dazer-waster, especially on our highways, and wrecking jobs, marriages and families into the millions. . . . pain-racked veterans of Korea and Vietnam given relief through addictive drugs, launching our nation's current drug crisis. . . . Scrabble. . . . runaways becoming child prostitutes. . . . soaring youthful suicides. . . . the back-lash search for answers - in faith; the Born-Agains, the Fundamentalists, Hari Krishnas, Moonies, "Jesus Freaks," etc. - or in self: Scientology, transcendental meditation, EST, analysis and psychotherapy, Rolfing, primal screams, the Me Decade, etc. - or answers in groups: communes, peer group counseling sessions for alcoholics, drug addicts, gamblers, batterers, widows, bringing together people with almost any common problem, finding comfort in numbers, but also groups like street gangs and even the murderous Manson "family". . . . the scorn for intellect - "pointy-heads" - the decline of erudition, vocabulary and grammar, even of basic reading and writing skills, the many functionally illiterate students and graduates of our high schools. . . . the celebration of mediocrity in popular arts. . . . the decline of the work ethic and aspiration. . . . the decline of personal and professional ethics, exposure of widespread chicanery among several Administrations' appointees causing mounting public cynicism toward public servants, doctors, lawyers and big business. . . . the downfall through scandal of many a sports idol.

. . . the national obsession with Jacqueline Kennedy Onassis. . . . graffiti. . . . the brutalization of society, our brutal movies, TV shows and newscast stories making mayhem and savagery commonplace, the mugging, rape and casual killing, copied by restless and alienated youths. . . . vanished safety in our streets, parks, stores and even homes, as random shootings spread, and the resultant arming of civilians for self-defense. . . . our perpetually overcrowded courts and prison system . . . . Cabbage Patch dolls. . . . the rise of terrorism to express social, political, or religious protest through bombings in the air (Pan Am) or on crowded land (New York's World Trade Center), skyjackings, hostage takings, etc. . . . . our domestic militant underground groups: AIM (American Indian Movement), Black Panthers, Weathermen, Symbionese Liberation Army, Jewish Defense League, neo-Nazis, Skin-Heads, and Ku Klux Klan, just a sampling. . . . skateboards and the return of roller skates, in the form of Rollerblades. . . . the total takeover by computers. . . . a whole revolution in communications, with push-button phones, cordless cellular, and car phones, answering machines, and fax. . . . bikinis. . . . the yearning for simple, down-home truths to relax our evermore complex lives, bringing an unprecedented popularity of country and western music. . . . our '60s big city ghetto riots in Los Angeles, Chicago, Washington, D.C., and Detroit. . . . Ladybird Johnson's floral beautification of Washington, D.C.. . . . scientists' warnings of felled rain forests, holes in the Ozone Layer, a greenhouse effect, global warming, all man-caused. . . . alerted Americans start multiple movements to save the environment; rain forests, whales, dolphins, baby seals - all endangered species of fauna and flora, to stop polluting and start recycling, in short, to save the planet and ourselves. . . . pet rocks . . . . home garbage disposals, automatic dishwashers, VCRs . . . . our (and the UN's) belated recognition of mainland China as China, rather than Nationalist China, (the island of Taiwan). . . . two more stars to our flag in 1959 as Alaska made our 49th state and Hawaii our 50th - Aloha!. . . . the loss of lovely national names like Persia, Ceylon, Rhodesia, Burma, Madagascar and the Congo, replaced by Iran, Sri Lanka, Zimbabwe, Myanmar, Malagasi Republic and Zaire. . . . those many former parts of the Soviet Union emerging as separate nation-states. . . . earlier struggles for freedom by Hungary in 1959, and by Czechoslovakia in 1968, brutally put down, (but stay tuned!). . . . another national obsession: Marilyn Monroe. . . . Entebbe. . . . Israel's astonishing record at making the desert bloom, and creating a viable, flourishing, cultural haven for all homeland-seeking Jews. . . .and Palestine Arabs still insisting on their homeland. . . . United Nations military action in the Congo. . . . Africa's ferment, old tribal quarrels flaring, once European colonial rule was lifted. . . . South Africa's Apartheid under increasing fire from the world community, and now dissolving through transition, not revolution. . . . under President Lyndon Johnson's prodding, Congress enacts much civil rights and War on Poverty legislation, the most social and economic remedies passed, since 1935. . . .India's Indira Gandhi, Israel's Golda Meier, the Philippines' Corazon Aquino, Britain's Margaret Thatcher, Sri Lanka's (Ceylon's) Sirimavo Bandaranaike, Ireland's Mary Robinson, Pakistan's Benazir Bhutto, and Nicaragua's Violeta Chamorro, showing the world that women can lead nations. . . . Watergate. . . . Richard Nixon, the only United States president to resign. . . . World Refugee Year, declared by the UN in 1960 to coax and shame governments into admitting their fair share of the 25 million displaced, stateless people still unsettled 15 years after World War II. . . . the frankness and courage of First Lady Betty Ford. . . . the Americans held hostage in Iran. . . . peacemaker President Jimmy Carter bringing Egypt's Anwar Sadat and Israel's Menachem Begin to Camp David, and the Nobel Peace Prize. . . . the reduction or dismantling, during the Reagan reign, of countless social and environmental programs, reversing forward strides, in the name of fiscal economy, while greatly swelling our arms appropriations. . . . just in that Administration's eight years, our National Debt more than *tripled:* from $907 billion, 701 million in 1980, to $2 trillion, 857 billion, 431 million by 1989. . . . stereo, transistor radios and tape recorders. . . . oil tankers and oil spills, topped by the Valdiz in Alaska. . . . chemical waste dumped into our waterways and seeping into our groundwater supply. . . . acid rain. . . . Three Mile Island. . . . solar energy, clean and full of promise - if not of profits. . . . the compact car and the foreign car takeover. . . . "planned obsolescence": deliberate shoddiness of manufacture, to insure early replacement; . . . Ralph Nader, leading the charge, as consumers rise up in self-defense. . . . Cappucino. . . . Women's Lib and NOW and ERA - the feminist movement, still with miles to go before it sleeps, but having come a long way, lady, and already having emptied many a home kitchen and nursery in favor of the work-for-pay place. . . . the persistent economic crunch requiring two-income households, to make ends meet; the resultant widespread demand for child care centers. . . . OPEC and its oily tyranny. . . . Frisbees. . . . our welcome of refugees from Hungary, Czechoslovakia, other Iron Curtain countries, Dutch-Indonesia, Vietnam, Laos, Cambodia, Cuba, El Salvador, Nicaragua, Haiti (sometimes), and more, all seeking a safer life. . . . and multitudes from Mexico and all Central America simply seeking a better life. . . . disco dancing, with its do-your-own-thing gyrations, often ignoring a partner. . . . the Pill and IUDs, the sexual revolution against traditional taboos. . . . changing life-styles to include unmarried couples living together, in such numbers that U.S. Census takers had to coin a new category for it: "POSS-L-Q" - (Persons of Opposite Sexes Sharing Living Quarters) - and "palimony" a court question, when POSS-L-Q doesn't work out. . . . singles bars. . . . "What's your sign?". . . . "swinging" couples. . . . sexually active adults, teens, adolescents and children, resulting in widespread exchange of venereal disease and in ignorant or careless pregnancies (over half a million unwanted pregnancies each year, just among teenage girls). . . . single mothers down to the age of 12, having and keeping their babies (87% of single adolescent mothers do). . . . despite 11,000,000 sexually active school-agers, loud outcries against any sex education in schools from parents who fail to teach their youngsters either restraint or precautions. . . . then as if those consequences of heedless sex, v.d., and pregnancy, were not enough of a heartbreak, along comes the tragedy of AIDS. . . . the dubious outcome of the Senate's Clarence Thomas/ Anita Hill hearings, and the emerging term: sexual harassment . . . . "Black is beautiful" and "I am somebody". . . . Chernobyl. . . . Bhopal. . . . after centuries of censure and secrecy, homosexuals move to declare themselves, "gays" emerging from their closets with dignity and/or gusto. . . . credit cards and the high interest price of instant gratification. . . . Roe vs. Wade, a rampart to defend or attack, dividing a nation over abortion; a right or a sin?. . . . groups calling themselves Right-to-Lifers, Operation Rescue and Lambs of Christ crowding and blocking access to clinics, preventing desperate women from obtaining legal abortions. . . . the wildfire spread of AIDS prompting the availability of condoms in some schools. . . . the thriving titillation business, in prime and soaptime TV, movies, advertising, dance, bars, tabloids, magazines and shops. . . . the cruel ravages of Thalidomide and Agent Orange. . . . frozen foods and home food freezers. . . . the international scramble for newly realized riches on the oceans' floor, and early gropings toward a universal Law of the Sea. . . . the national health and fitness zeal, reflected in reformed smokers, calorie counters, cholesterol spurners, health food stores, crowded gyms, home work out videos, walk-a-thons, bike-a-thons and joggers across the land. . . . "Paper or plastic?", "For here or to go?", "Smoking or non-smoking?", "Your place or mine?", "Have a nice day", "Wait for the beep". . . Colombia's government defying, immensely rich, powerful and ruthless drug lords. . . . Australia's steady growth in population, industry, economy and culture. . . . China's harsh takeover of Tibet, and the Dalai Lama still in exile. . . . the shoes of Imelda Marcos. . . .El Salvador's long, anguished civil war and later, the UN Truth Commission's findings of Government guilt for atrocities. . . . Nicaragua's elected socialist regime, the Sandinistas, and right-wing Americans' covert backing of the "Contras". . . . Oliver North and the Iran-Contra scandal. . . . "pooper-scoopers" for city sidewalk dog walkers. . . . microwave ovens. . . . our national disgrace: the homeless, a growing population in cities, suburbs and the countrysides, millions now, with nowhere they belong, and no national plan to rescue or just to shelter them. . . . paintings by big-name masters fetching dozens of millions of dollars at auction. . . . American billionaires (people with a thousand millions of dollars or more). . . . aerobics. . . . boat people, the desperate emigrés from Vietnam and Haiti, many drowning at sea, or ravaged by pirates; those who survive and reach shore often pushed back out to sea or penned up in camps indefinitely. . . . white wine and Perrier newly preferred to cocktails and highballs at social events. . . . one-parent U.S. households now outnumbering our two-parent ones. . . . ever more job-holding single parents, leaving their children in the care of others, or on their own (latchkey kids). . . . school dropouts. . . . growing vandalism and arson. . . . the exposure of widespread wife and child abuse, and the establishment of safe havens for victims, and jail or therapy for abusers. . . . marriage and family counseling. . . . and finally! courses in "parenting" training. . . . telephone "Hot Lines" for the desperate and despairing. . . . the Las Vegas Strip: glitz, greed and girls. . . . Trivial Pursuit. . . . the Ayatollah Khomeini, apostle of hate. . . . the new diet must: fibre. . . . pizzas. . . . pasta. . . . all of Cambodia a killing field, the Kmer Rouge savagely scourging those gentle people of their intellectuals. . . . and earlier, China's demented "Cultural Revolution". . . . more American women seeking and winning public office. . . . violent crime every 17 seconds in the U.S. . . . . John F. Kennedy, Robert Kennedy, Martin Luther King, Anwar Sadat and John Lennon shot and killed; Ronald Reagan, George Wallace and Pope John Paul shot; Gerald Ford shot at. . . . the Gun Lobby (National Rifle Association) very large. . . . the Handgun Control movement very small - but growing - in the wake of repeated mass slaughter with automatic rifles, by deranged or disgruntled killers. . . . there are now more licensed gun dealers than gas stations in the U.S. . . . . getting your money at an ATM can also get you shot. . . . .teenage gangs' gun warfare on city streets, drive-by shots felling pedestrians and children at play. . . . seven Los Angeles residents currently dying each day from gunshots. . . . and as our society slips backward, our technology keeps leaping forward: MRI, magnetic resonant imaging, brings a medical breakthrough in diagnosis; and virtual reality, a futuristic marvel, here today, projecting one's self into a computer-generated artificial world . . . Wall Street insider trading scandals. . . . junk bonds and the financial wreckage they caused. . . . the epidemic of savings and loans' failures, and banks as well, with government takeovers. . . . the astronomic bill it will cost the U.S. taxpayers to make good these losses, caused by corrupt or inept bank officials, mostly unpunished. . . . and BCCI, Bank of Credit & Commerce International, ("Bank of Crooks & Criminals"), an evil network of drugs, weapons and money laundering, and massive thievery affecting 69 countries. . . . alone among former U.S. presidents, Jimmy Carter devotes himself to helping others. . . . Mikhail Gorbachev, miracle worker who changes the world, daring to point out the failures of Soviet Communism. . . . the Soviet Union's economic crisis, the folly of the Cold War, and its bankrupting arms race . . . . Gorbachev opening Soviet society with programs called Perestroika and Glasnost. . . . these reforms embolden the people of many Iron Curtain countries to insist on greater freedoms, and almost bloodlessly, Poland, Czechoslovakia, Hungary, Romania, Bulgaria and Albania are restored to self-determination. . . . the Berlin Wall comes down (1961 - 1989). . . . even in China, a spirited but peaceful bid for greater freedom erupts, but is put down ruthlessly by the government at Tiananmen Square. . . . greater freedom after 74 years of Communism, the USSR simply dissolves before an astonished world, leaving no clear plan to succeed it. . . . and the 15 states that comprised it grope their way toward full, separate nationhood or membership in a shaky Commonwealth of Independent States, squabbling among themselves over old grievances and how to apportion that huge area's resources, industries and services. . . . an abortive coup by die-hard Stalinists is put down by the people of Moscow, led by Boris Yeltsin, who then becomes President of Russia. . . . and the man who brought about all this new freedom, Mikhail Gorbachev, is no longer in power or office. . . . the World Health Organization, (WHO) reports that the global spread of the AIDS virus must now be termed pandemic, affecting men, women and children on all continents, with a cumulative total of victims since 1981 projected to be 30 to 40 million people by the year 2,000. . . . other wars, other places: Israel, Britain and France seize and then release the Suez Canal, Algeria wrests independence from France, all Israeli/Arab wars in the Middle East; Northern Ireland's deadly bid for independence from Britain; Cyprus; Indonesia; Sri Lanka . . . . Nigeria, Namibia, Somalia just an African cauldron-sampling, Lebanon's Beirut reduced to rubble by faction fanatics, Britain/Argentina, over the Falkland Islands, Iran and Iraq try to destroy each other; civil wars in Afghanistan, Ethiopia, Sudan, ex-Yugoslavia, just a few. . . . is mankind incurably warlike?. . . . our military moves since the Bay of Pigs and Vietnam: Libya, Lebanon, Grenada, Panama, (invading and arresting its elected president, Noriega, bringing him to trial and imprisonment on U.S. soil) and then "Desert Shield and Desert Storm" against Iraq. . . . (and what did any of those countries do to us, to provoke our hostile action?). . .

with the Cold War's end, the ex-Soviets and we step back from the nuclear abyss as disarmament proceeds to everyone's relief. . . . the resurgent hope that the United Nations can bring the planet together and keep it together. . . . Biosphere 2, a sealed, self-sustaining mini-world. . . . fiber-optics. . . . digital technologies creating a communicopia of entertainment, information and interactive services . . . . U.S., the world's richest country, now its biggest debtor: just the 1992 deficit is $358 billion, . . . authorities won't tell how many $billions the Persian Gulf War cost us, but in US forces' lives it's 374 and who knows how many other fellow-humans? The guess is 100,000 Iraqis killed . . . . the rise and spread of Islamic fundamentalism . . . our national debt now climbing towards $5 trillion, a sum 5 times what it was at the start of the Reagan reign in 1980, . . . repeating history, just as the '30s Depression followed the "Wheee!" years of the '20s, so now in the '90s, we pay dearly for the "Greed is Good!" years of the '80s. . . . and while our defeated ex-foes, Germany and Japan thrive, the U.S. slumps badly, in a recession penetrating and stubborn. . . . massive lay-offs and plant closures or moves abroad, giant industries leave, merge, fold or go bankrupt, such as store-chains and airlines, rampant foreclosures, and government services cut back just when needed most, as income revenues dwindle. . . . "trickle-down" economics didn't, under Reagan or Bush, and finally the greatly lowered middle class opts for a real change with Clinton and Gore, a team both competent and caring; revived hope fills the air . . . . Los Angeles suffers the largest insurrection in modern times in reaction to the Rodney King verdict, an enemy air strike could scarcely have wrought more damage and suffering . . . . In Florida, hurricane Andrew inflicts the costliest wreckage of all U.S. natural disasters . . . . 15 years apart, religious followers of two fanatical cult leaders are dead; by poison in Jim Jones' "Jamestown," Guyana, and by

fire in David Koresh's "Branch Dividian" compound near Waco, Texas. . . . after centuries of wars and hostile competition, 12 nations, having joined forces to create the Common Market, are now launching the European Economic Community, (EEC), for common benefit. . . . and now the North American Free Trade Agreement . . . . the pervasive spread of television and its immense influence on all our lives, bringing Olympic Games, political conventions and candidates' debates, beauty contests, symphonies, game shows, ballets, talk-shows, cooking classes, variety shows, sermons, Academy Awards, every sport's contest: football, basketball, baseball, hockey, boxing, golf, and tennis, satellite launchings and moon landings, cartoons, old movies, sitcoms, westerns, horror shows, documentaries, soap operas by day and by night, newscasts and weather reports, assassinations, riots and wars (always interspersed by commercials) right into our homes to digest, along with our meals and snacks. . . . our growing awareness of the outside world, of its ferment - creating millions of refugees - awareness of hunger that weakens half a billion people . . . . of mass starvation in Somalia's terrorized, leaderless, ravaged land. U.S. troops sent halfway around the world, not to kill in combat, but to protect and save. International forces join in the effort . . . . And in what was Yugoslavia, old hatreds flare into vicious assaults on cities and civilians. Faced with that awful suffering and the likely spread of hostilities, the world community stirs to intervene . . . . And a great, continuous outpouring of food and medicine to distant strangers in distress, from private citizens in many lands, channels their help through a network of religious and private agencies.

Since compassion surely is a measure of civilization, it's comforting to see how our species, for all its faults, grows in compassion. 🐦

Summation

Having read this far, just contemplating what has befallen us since 1950 could make you conclude that mankind is a downhill racer, hurtling rapidly toward self-destruction at rock bottom. Certainly there's enough here to make us sigh, shake our heads, wipe a tear and grind our teeth, more than enough. And yet, if we search, and we do have to, we can find a number of things to cheer about.

All the same, there's no denying that right now our own nation is in deep trouble, entirely of our own making, and it will take inspired leadership and some time, with all of us pulling together to haul it out and set it on a straight course again. We can, and of course we will, because we must. We've done it before.

But what has that long, long list of changes and trends, blessings and curses since mid-century to do with "The Way We Wore"? Nothing and everything, I'd say. Just trying to make our way through the thicket of challenges besetting us from day to day, who among us still had time to devote to leisurely shopping, lengthy fittings and a bird-dog search for just the right accessories? Not I, for one. Most of us have settled for more casual comfort and clothes that fill many functions. If we don formal attire two or three times within a year, it's a banner year, and the occasions memorable.

What were we wearing in the four decades since 1950? Well, let's see. At first we were very feminine in our full, billowing skirts with ruffled petticoats. Role models were Loretta Young, Harriet Nelson, Jane Wyatt and Donna Reed, wholesome as can be on TV. Coifs became bouffant, our hair back-combed, high, wide and awesome, making our heads look half again their true size, and murder to sit behind at a movie.

I can remember empire high waistlines, A-line dresses and sheaths, all looking superb on Audrey Hepburn. With the '60s onset of the Beatles came a link to England, and London's Carnaby Street far-out styles caught on locally. Young girls assembled costumes of oddly assorted period lace and velvet, often charming.

Why, during and since the '60s, did the young spurn conventional dress and adopt blue jeans? In the midst of all that turmoil, and furious over having an "immoral war" foisted on them, many found The Establishment, all over 30, hypocritical and alien, and refused to conform to their dress codes. They preferred rigidly conforming to their own chosen uniform of "non-conformity," for all occasions. Levis also provided a social-economic leveler, since nearly all could afford them, and the young were opting for a classless society. An Afro hairdo signified racial pride. Unkempt long hair, beards, sometimes bare feet and general scruffiness all were signs of rebellion and of youthful contempt for grooming as "square." Girls and guys alike let long, lank hair just hang there, parting those curtains that hid their eyes only when it was vital to see or be seen. Since most were slender, viewed from the rear, a uni-sex look took over, so that only frontal contours divulged a him-or-her identity.

I can recall a fad for paper dresses and a spate of space-age, angular, aggressive-looking outfits, could they have coincided with Helen Reddy singing "I Am Woman, Hear Me Roar!"? of which rage only the boots have survived, worn still, perhaps because they were such an investment. Then there were the square-toed, boxy, clunky shoes, looking too heavy to lift for the next step. Then there were platform shoes, the despair of short dates, unless they too, got a lift underfoot. And while we're including men, let's not forget the bell-bottom pants, which lasted a decade, or Nehru jackets, which didn't. Ties widened and narrowed almost with the seasons.

We can't forget the Bikini bare minimum sun-and-see suit, because it's still with us, though less and less of it each year. Came the miniskirt for those whose legs warrant such display - and at the moment, it's back, briefer than ever, if possible - but also, there are much longer hemlines, midcalf and even just topping the ankle, for day wear as well as after dark. You can now please yourself, a comfy state of affairs. Twiggy, the reed-slim model, drove hordes of women onto diets, and even now, 60 million Americans are on reducing programs. That's 1 of every 4 of us.

With the fitness kick came jogging suits, often in stunning jewel tones of velour, and worn for many other pursuits than jogging by both men and women. Their comfort was too good to resist. Speaking of comfort, women in droves discarded their bras, opting for the natural (if less perky) look, spurred on by Women's Liberation Movement. The desired bustline has heaved up and down, more or less, over these years. Breast implants became widespread, as underendowed women strove to look more fetching to men. But now the risks of implants are known, haunting the implanted, and daunting the not-yet.

Great, oversized sweaters, kaftans and muumuus, for those who prefer to hide their contours, or just to be comfortable. Then there's the blouson torso, totally disguising one's shape, all but the emphasized hips. Jumpsuits are another co-ed style, as are "sweats" workout togs, now as commonly seen in Southern California as jogging suits. The layered look, and the return of shoulder pads, back for a decade now. Years of heavy make-up, ballerina-style, and years of almost none. Pointed toe shoes are back, to cripple a whole new generation. At last, women are opting for low heels by day, saving high heels for after dark. Culottes and walking shorts are with us once more. Just now, a craze is upon us, called the "grunge" look. As lovely as its name, it mis-assembles apparel items, as tacky and clashy as possible. A prankish nose-thumbing at established, tidy norms of appearance, it's probably fun for a while. But not to worry; this, too, will pass.

The '80s saw a return to glamour and a flaunting of wealth. Today, what with the recession and many robberies, there's more discretion in showing off riches, except in cars. Grander ones are stolen and driven away after a gunpoint confrontation, prompting a new term: car-jacking, and it's widespread.

Big, bravura costume jewelry is popular and acceptable everywhere just now, both genders sharing this trend, along with pierced ears. The last few years, huge, showy earrings have appeared, dangling not just at very dressy functions, but at work, often preferred over any other jewelry. Here, Jane Fonda was a trail-blazer, as she was with fitness workouts. Fewer and fewer furs are seen anywhere these days, a triumph for the animal rights advocates. As more and more people travel frequently, "packing light" has become the watchword. They choose a few interchangeable separates, to combine into seemingly many outfits.

Reading over that list of post - '40s style trends, I see a whole lot of things that didn't last. Of course, fashion isn't meant to last, is it? We're meant to have to buy whole new wardrobes every little while. That's what keeps America's "rag-trade" going. Fair enough. Oddly, though, it strikes me that the clothes shown in this book would look acceptable not only now, 50 years after they originated, but also in most of the years between then and now. They're quite timeless, these clothes. On the other hand, I think that most of the styles <u>since</u> then would look out of place at any time other than their own - which perhaps justifies putting together this picture show of Things from Then to focus our attention on a period of grace and charm.

I guess we all must agree that 1950, this 20th century's halfway point, did indeed mark the end of an era, an era of continuity, such as we may never know again. It was an era that each of us old enough will remember differently, but one I greatly relished experiencing, and have truly enjoyed leafing through again, with you. ❦

Hollywood Fights Back!

Congress shall make no law respecting an establishment of religion, or prohibiting the free exercise thereof; or abridging the freedom of speech or of the press; or the right of the people peaceably to assemble and to petition the Government for a redress of grievances.

-- The First Amendment to Constitution of the United States.

We, the undersigned, as American citizens who believe in constitutional democratic government, are disgusted and outraged by the continuing attempt of the House Committee on Un-American Activities to smear the Motion Picture Industry.

We hold that these hearings are morally wrong because:

Any investigation into the political beliefs of the individual is contrary to the basic principles of our democracy;

Any attempt to curb freedom of expression and to set arbitrary standards of Americanism is in itself disloyal to both the spirit and the letter of our constitution.

Robert Ardrey
Stephen Morehouse Avery
Robert Alterman
Judith Alden
Larry Adler

Lucille Ball
John Beal
Leonardo Bercovici
Charles Boyer
Geraldine Brooks
Humphrey Bogart
Lauren Bacall
Richard Brooks
Sidney Buchman
Si Bartlett
Joan Bennett
Barbara Bentley
DeWitt Bodeen
Steve Brown
Peter Beeger
Edith Barrett
Leonard Bernstein
Roma Burton
Ann & Mort Braus
Millen Brand
George Bassman
Abe Burrows
Henry Branden
Irving Brecher
Michael Blankfort
Ethel Barrymore

McClure Capps
Warren Cowan
Frank Caliendar
Eddie Cantor
Richard Conte
Norman Corwin
Loretta Carlson
Morris Cohn
Lee Carrau
Frank Conlan
Anne P. Carie
Ellen Corby
Louis Calhern
Mr. and Mrs. Edward Cahn
Rose Cooper
Edward Clark
Jerome Chodorov
Cheryl Crawford
Tom Carlyle

Armand Deutsch
Jay Dratler
Kirk Douglas
Gerold Dolan
Philip Dunne
I. A. L. Diamond
Walter Doniger
Spencer Davies
Donald Davies
Delmer Daves
Muni Diamond
Howard Duff
Paul Draper
Agnes DeMille
Deanna Durbin

Melvyn Douglas
Jules Dassin
Valentine Davies
Howard Dimsdale
Ludwig Donath
Howard DaSylva
Arthur J. Daly

Julius J. Epstein
Philip G. Epstein
William Eythe
Florence Eldridge
Henry & Phoebe Ephron

Melvyn Frank
Joseph Fields
Margaret Francis
Daniel Fuchs
Henry Fonda
Joel Fluellen
Bernard Fein
Bob Fine
Sylvia Fine
Ketti Frings
Harriet Franks, Jr.
Arlene Francis
Mr. & Mrs. Felix Feist

John Garfield
Ava Gardner
Sheridan Gibney
Paulette Goddard
Benny Goodman
Michael Gordon
Henry Gordon
Jack Goodman
Johnny Green
S. L. Gomberg
Erwin Gelsey
Madeline Gesas
Jay Goldburg
Judy Garland
Jesse J. Goldburg
Jimmy Gleason
Ruth Gorgon
Barbara Bel Geddes
Milton M. Grossman
Bonnie Green
Rhoda Gibson
Saks A. Goodman
Betty Garret
Sheila Graham
Robert Grosvenor
Dorothy Gibbs
Gus Gale
Doris Grau
Ira Gershwin

Henry Hathaway
Richard Hale
Van Heflin
Paul Henreid
Katharine Hepburn
John Houseman
Marsha Hunt
John Huston
Harold Hecht
June Havoc

Sterling Hayden
Moss Hart
Uta Hagen
Rita Hatworth
David Hopkins
Joseph Hoffman
Ben Hecht
Celeste Holm
Roberta Harrison
David Hertz
Walter Huston
William Holden
Arthur Hornblow, Jr.

Arthur Jacobs
Alvin Josephy
Robert L. Joseph
Felix Jackson

Peter W. Klain
Arthur Kober
Evelyn Keyes
Norman Krasna
Lester Koenig
Herbert Kline
Michael Kraike
Danny Kaye
J. Arthur Kennedy
Isobel Katleman
J. Richard Kennedy
Fred Kohlmar
Ethel Kurlaso
Fay and Michael Kanin
Garson Kanin
George Kaufman
Gene Kelly
George S. Kaufman

Canada Lee
Herbert C. Lewis
Arthur Lubin
M. C. Levee, Jr.
Fritz Lang
Burt Lancaster
M. C. Levee
Bernie Lay
Anatole Litvak
Myrna Loy
Mary Anita Loos
Frank Loesser
Melvin & Margaret Levy
Peter Lorre
Frank Liverman
Lee Loeb
Ted Loeff

Richard Maibaum
Frank L. Moss
Margo
Ivan Moffatt
Joseph Mischel
Dorothy Mathews
David Miller
Gene Markey
Fredric March Groucho Marx
Henry Morgan
Audie Murphy
Rouben Mamoulian

Sarah Jane Miles
Irwin Meltzer
Martin Mason
Buddy Murry
I. Markin
Margaret Muse
Weldon Morgan
Carol Morris
Danial Mainwaring
Burgess Meredith
Dorothy McGuire
Dorothy Miles Colin Miller
Archibald Macleish
Gummo Marx
Ronald Mintz
Vincent Minnelli
Robert McCahon

Lorie Niblo
Richard N. Nash
Marsha Norman
Dorris Nolan
Robert Nathan

M. Offner
George Oppenheimer

Marion Parsonnet
Robert Presnell, Jr.
Joseph PasternakErnest
Pascal
Barbara & James Poe
Robert Pirnosh
Gregory Peck
M. C. Preve
Vincent Price
Bob Pryor
Stanley M. Pearson
Pat Patterson
Frank Partos
Blossom Plumb
Norman Panama
Abe Polansky
John Paxton

Mary Rapp
Robert Ryan
Edward G. Robinson
Earl Robinson
Henry C. Rogers
Irving Ravetch
Irving Reis
Gladys Robinson
Francis Rosenwald
Irving Rubine
Sylvia Richards
Norman & Betsy Rose
Harold Rome
Donna Reed
Ann Revere
Nicholas Ray
Lyle Rooks

George Seaton
Steve Sekely
LaVerne Shaffner
Carol Stone
Allen Scott

Dr. Harlow Shapley
Artie Shaw
Joseph Sistrom
Shepperd Strudwick
Robert Siodmak
Arthur Strawn
Robert Shapiro
Irwin Shaw
John & Marti Shelton
Milton Sperling
Barry Sullivan
John Stone
Theodore Strauss
Mrs. Leo Spitz
Frank Sinatra
Sylvia Sidney
Taft Shreiber
L. M. Salvo, Jr.
Billy Smith
Kenny Starr
Milton Starr
Robert Sale
Bob Spears

Jane Turner
Leo Townsend
Claire Trevor
Franchot Tone
Aimee Torriani
Felix Terry
Wanda Tynan
Joseph Than
David S. Treffman
Sophie Tucker
Lawrence Edmund Taylor

Michael Uris
Don Victor
Bernard Vorhaus
Benay Venuta
Mrs. Frieda Victor

Walter Wanger
Cornel Wilde
Bill Watters
Keenan Wynn
William Wyler
Orson Welles
Charles Winninger
Jane Wyatt
Pinky Wilson
Billy Wilder
Carleton Wiggins
Jerry Wald
Patricia R. Woods
GeorgeWoods
Pat Walker
Anne Wigton
William Wright
Robert Young
Irving Yergin
Collier Young
Sam Zimbalist
Also four U.S. Senators:
Harley Kilgore, W. Va.
Claude Pepper, Fla.
Elbert Thomas, Utah
Glen Taylor, Idaho

Committee For The First Amendment & Bill Of Rights

(This page is reproduced from the 1947 Committee Presentation)

Marsha Hunt
Filmography

Paramount Contract

The Virginia Judge (1935)
The Accusing Finger (1936)
Gentle Julia (1936) - (loan out, 20th Century-Fox)
Desert Gold (1936)
Arizona Raiders (1936)
Hollywood Boulevard (1936)
College Holiday (1937)
Easy To Take (1936)
Murder Goes To College (1937)
Born To The West (1937) - *(aka Hell Town)*
Easy Living (1937)
Thunder Trail (1937)
Annapolis Salute (1937) - (loan out, RKO)

Free Lance

Come On, Leathernecks (1938) - Republic
The Long Shot (1938) - Grand National
The Star Reporter (1939) - Monogram
The Hardys Ride High (1939) - MGM
These Glamour Girls (1939) - MGM
*Joe & Ethel Turp Call On The
  President* (1939) - MGM
Winter Carnival (1939) - United Artists
Irene - (1940) - RKO
Women In Hiding (1940) - MGM
Ellery Queen, Master Detective (1940) - Monogram
Flight Command (1940) - MGM
Pride And Prejudice (1940) - MGM
The Trial Of Mary Dugan (1941) - MGM
Cheers For Miss Bishop (1941) - United Artists

Paramount Contract:	1935 - 1938
Free-Lance:	1938 - 1941
MGM Contract:	1941 - 1946
Free-Lance:	1946 -

NOTE: Film dates given by Miss Hunt
were production shooting years. A film's
release/distribution date was often the following year.

Metro-Goldwyn-Mayer Contract

The Penalty (1941)
I'll Wait For You (1941)
Blossoms In The Dust (1941)
Unholy Partners (1941)
Panama Hattie (1942)
Joe Smith, American (1942)
The Affairs Of Martha (1942)
Seven Sweethearts (1942)
Kid Glove Killer (1942)
Pilot #5 (1943)
Thousands Cheer (1943)
Cry Havoc! (1943)
Lost Angel (1943)
The Human Comedy (1943)
Bride By Mistake (1944) - (loan out, RKO)
None Shall Escape (1944) - (loan out, Columbia)
Music For Millions (1944)
The Valley Of Decision (1945)
A Letter For Evie (1945)
Smash-Up (1947) - (loan-out, Universal)

Free Lance

Carnegie Hall (1947) - United Artists
The Inside Story (1948) - Republic
Raw Deal (1948) - Eagle-Lion
Jigsaw (1949) - United Artists
Take One False Step (1949) - Universal
Mary Ryan, Detective (1950) - Columbia
Actors And Sin (1952) - United Artists
The Happy Time (1952) - Columbia
Diplomatic Passport (1954) - Eros
No Place To Hide (1956) - Allied Artists
Bombers B-52 (1957) - Warner Brothers
Back From The Dead (1957) - 20th Century-Fox
Blue Denim (1959) - 20th Century-Fox
The Plunderers (1960) - Allied Artists
Johnny Got His Gun (1971) - Cinemation

Index

(Apparel Index Follows)

Apparel Index

T: top   L: left
C: center   R: right
B: bottom